Clinton Ross

Chalmette

The History of the Adventures & Love Affairs of Captain Robe Before & During the Battle of

New Orleans

Clinton Ross

Chalmette
The History of the Adventures & Love Affairs of Captain Robe Before & During the Battle of New Orleans

ISBN/EAN: 9783743399440

Manufactured in Europe, USA, Canada, Australia, Japa

Cover: Foto ©ninafisch / pixelio.de

Manufactured and distributed by brebook publishing software (www.brebook.com)

Clinton Ross

Chalmette

THAT BALCONY CORNER IS EVER TO BE HELD DEAR

Page 219.

CHALMETTE

THE HISTORY OF THE ADVENTURES & LOVE AFFAIRS OF CAPTAIN ROBE BEFORE & DURING THE BATTLE OF NEW ORLEANS: WRITTEN BY HIMSELF

BY CLINTON ROSS

AUTHOR OF "THE SCARLET COAT," "ZULEKA," ETC.

PHILADELPHIA & LONDON
J. B. LIPPINCOTT COMPANY
1898

TO

ADMIRAL ERBEN

MY DEAR ADMIRAL,—You, sir, have borne the American flag on so many seas,—in so many affairs,—before so many peoples,—that I venture to put your name,—distinguished in the service of the United States,—before this tale of Chalmette.

What finer introduction could it have, though indeed but a landsman's tale? Yet I may hesitate; for who may spin a yarn better than yourself? who knows so well how to fascinate with some rare account? who may see more readily the faults, the incongruities of my attempt? May I hope that your name will prove the talisman which shall command for " Chalmette" some favor?

I am, sir
Yours faithfully
CLINTON ROSS

At NEW YORK, 27th April, '97

CLASS NO.	AUTHOR Ross, Clinton		L. C. CARD NUMBER
	TITLE Chalmette		
ACC. NO.			
LIST PRICE	PLACE Phila.	PUBLISHER Lippincott	YEAR 1898
DEALER	VOLS.	SERIES	EDITION
NO. OF COPIES 1	RECOMMENDED BY	DATE ORDERED 6/4/64	COST
ORDER NO.	FUND CHARGED UCLA dup.	DATE RECEIVED	

**UNIVERSITY OF CALIFORNIA LIBRARY
IRVINE, CALIFORNIA**

AUTHOR'S NOTE

Three books on cities stand out preëminent for charm of subject and grace of manner,— D'Amicis's "Constantinople," Stevenson's "Edinboro," and Miss King's "New Orleans;" and to this last I must acknowledge my debt

CONTENTS

CHAPTER I
Christopher Robe visits Westmore . . . 15

CHAPTER II
New Orleans 36

CHAPTER III
Mademoiselle de Renier 59

CHAPTER IV
The Letter 65

CHAPTER V
The Pirates of Barataria 75

CHAPTER VI
The Ward of Lafitte and Captain Dominique You 91

CHAPTER VII
The Death-Bed of De Bertrand . . . 104

CONTENTS

CHAPTER VIII
    The Entertainment to his Majesty's Officers 110

CHAPTER IX
    The Diplomacy of Lafitte 119

CHAPTER X
    Monsieur Clement 129

CHAPTER XI
    The Ursuline Sister 143

CHAPTER XII
    The Entrance of the Prince 156

CHAPTER XIII
    At Madame Demarche's 171

CHAPTER XIV
    Lafitte and the Traitor 184

CHAPTER XV
    The Escape 198

CHAPTER XVI
    The Balcony at Madame Demarche's . . 206

CONTENTS

CHAPTER XVII

The First Days of the Battle 225

CHAPTER XVIII

The Rivals 232

CHAPTER XIX

Other Days of Battle 236

CHAPTER XX

The Eighth of January 240

CHAPTER XXI

The Quarrel of M. Jean Lafitte and Captain Robe 249

PREFATORY NOTE

That my dear grandfather was one of the first men of his time, I dare say I need not state. The achievements of Christopher Robe are too obvious before those who read the histories of Americans. And so I need not apologize too much for presenting here his own account of his life. 'Tis, in fact, a matter of pride to me to serve him in the poor way of editor. He did so much in these United States,—in those days that are now so far away as to be matters of tradition,—that his own history of these great events,—particularly of General Jackson and the battle of New Orleans and of the pirates of Barataria,—may be accepted as a book of more than the private interest to us, who are his kin.

I have followed for the most his own phrasing; the manuscript is as it was found in the old house by the Potomac. And the editor has only touched it here and there,—with a reverential hand,—since he was the most distinguished of her race. I may add here that I have a very vivid memory of him as I saw him when, a girl, I was brought back from Europe to Westmore. My memory pictures a stretch of lawn and an old man very well kept, with bright eyes,—they were, I believe, intensely black,—two great hounds by his side. He paused and exchanged a laughing remark with the little girl who was watching him almost wonderingly. For she had seen his name and his picture in a very bad wood-cut in a history of the United States. He was, I remember, a small man, yet he ever carried himself with a certain air which gave him distinction. When younger he was said to have been very muscular, and in his old age he possessed an air of great strength. And I am reminded of that portrait of him, taken when he was a general of the Mexican War, which showed him strong and virile; a thin, fine, smooth-shaven face, framed by brown hair; a short, compact figure; a hand,

PREFATORY NOTE   xv

slender and nervous, on his sword. He looked every inch like those men of our line of whom Stuart and Peale have left several famous likenesses.

When the girl saw him that day it was, I think, in '57. He died in '59, before that terrible civil strife which divided our family. The question was never put to him,—the Union or the Confederation? His life ended before that. But he belonged to another splendid period of American history, when our nationality asserted itself lustily, when we were felt as one of the naval powers to be counted on, when Great Britain found it not so easy a matter to force her former colonies back into their parts in the British Empire. 'Tis a story of many events that may make us feel shame,—of incompetency, of poor politics,—but out of it all comes the splendid distinction of the American navy and of the fight General Jackson made at New Orleans.

But I am possibly saying too much of this manuscript of my dear grandfather. I will leave it, without further apology, to speak for itself, as if he himself were talking. And why, indeed, isn't he? The lines were penned by him, and here on my desk lie the papers as he left them in those last quiet days at Westmore.

CORNELIA ROBE FENWOLD.

AT WESTMORE, VIRGINIA,
   7th April, 1897.

CHALMETTE

CHAPTER I

CHRISTOPHER ROBE VISITS WESTMORE

The writer of this reminiscence heard the great American's Farewell Address; a little lad that day, standing by his uncle's side, the scene still made an impression that he carried down into other years; and when in the period of our inefficiency we said American traditions were lost,—when they had won the fights in the West and burned Washington,—the man and the lad recalled that other scene. Kit remembers how the uncle and nephew walked together side by side, the elder talking vehemently, as was his habit, recalling what Kit's father had done in the former war.

"But the navy has done its part well, Kit," he added; "we were even going to curtail that,—in our idea to economize." And Mr. Robe went into a tirade about the ways and means of politicians. Now, as a matter of observation, Kit is sure that the same old tirades are being constantly delivered against politicians and parties. 'Tis ever a discussion, a quarrel, this struggle we have in the world; and 'twas the same in 1814 as now. What could be better, or worse, than a certain course? What a villain is that leader! how are the people bought and sold, or led astray! how much better were our fathers in their day and generation! And so the discussion goes on endlessly, and the old world keeps jogging on, jogging on.

"I think well of your expedition to New Orleans, Kit, but I don't see how Louisiana is to be saved to us. What can Andrew Jackson, indeed, do? It's their last resort, and it's a notice to the Louisianians,—take care of yourselves, and we will approve. Think of those veterans of the Peninsula,—those leaders who burned the Capitol only the other day; and I could see the flames rising over the hills. I sat there in the library and wanted to have my legs again,—as I used to be before the gout took 'em away from me. But you've done passably well, Kit," he added; " and it's good of you to come around to see me before you go down there."

Mr. Robe then went on talking about the particulars of the estate, which some day was to be Kit's all, things turning out properly. The Robe name, the Robe career,—were the nephew's to follow after him. They paused over Kit's father's portrait as they talked, and Kit looked across to his mother's, which faced it. They died within a year of each other, in '91, when Kit was five. John Robe, the boy's guardian and uncle, looked after him; he had never married, and Kit appeared to be his main interest, his care. Kit can see him now as they stood there talking together,—the best friends in the world; nothing seemed ever likely to come between them, except one subject: a woman. The uncle knew quite as well as any one that part of the reason for the nephew being at Robe House, on his way down to New

Orleans, was that, as you follow the river, you come to the plantation of the Maurices. The uncle held the Maurices not of so good blood; and he had his certain fears about Sallie Maurice and Christopher Robe. What good guardian quite approves of one's choice of a woman? and a father, or an uncle like Kit's, who took a father's place, cherishes the illusion that no one in the world is quite the equal of their particular boy. Kit recalls how he left him, finding some excuse, and rode with Simon Wesley, his boy, across to the Maurices.

It was a quiet, charming day, and though Virginia had been stirred and frightened out of her wits by the recent invasion, there was no evidence of unrest or war that moment. The chatter of the fields reached Captain Robe pleasantly; a rhythm of summer lay about on the slopes. Now and then he had to stop to speak to some darky who was glad indeed to see him back from the wars. And then suddenly, about a turn, he came on her walking by her horse,—as his luck would have it.

CHALMETTE 19

"Sallie," said he, dismounting.

"Ah, it's Kit," she cried; "Kit, you're back then."

Sallie Maurice was neither tall nor short; as Kit remembers that moment, of a rather full figure, an eager, smiling face framed by reddish-brown hair. Now, as she stood by the roadside, her face flushed slightly at the sight of the young captain. Was she glad to see him back? Had she heard he had gained a captaincy at Lundy's Lane? All the little vanities he had about himself—and I don't believe he had more than most men—asserted themselves. But surely he had never found in his wanderings a prettier, more winsome face than this Virginia maid's, with that rarely piquant grace. He wondered if the two Braytons,—Tom and Sam, cousins, proprietors of Westmoreland,—were still so persistent suitors as they had been. Was he too late, then? Had others taken her fancy? For as they stood there our captain was suddenly in a fever of interest.

"Do you remember when we last met?"

said he, sillily enough, looking not at her, but at the river making a broad sweep with splendid grandeur at their feet. The great rivers, the Hudson, the Potomac, the Mississippi, seem to typify the strength and virility of the United States.

"That night at Mrs. Madison's," Sally said, laughing rather mischievously. "Poor Mrs. Madison had such a hard time when they ran away from Washington," she added, as if wishing to change the subject. And then Kit noticed that she looked paler than when he had seen her last. In his pleasure at seeing her face he had not noted that, and now he asked, rather anxiously,—

"Why, where's all your color, old playmate?"

But as he said it her face was suffused again with a rush of crimson.

"I surely have enough now," said she, her eyes bent down, "to please you, sir. Well I may be paler. My uncle says that I am worried."

"What in the world can worry you?" he cried; "a love-affair?" he added, with attempted facetiousness. "Eh, Sallie? You'd become so popular even before I left."

"I care not for men," she said, with an upward look belying the statement. "If that were all that could bother me, I should not have a care in the world. And how do you do, Simon Wesley?" she said, calling to the boy. "How well you look,—almost as well as your master, the captain."

"Simon is a soldier," said Kit then, while Simon rolled his eyes and showed his glittering teeth.

"He's been in a mile of bullets," the master went on, and Simon turned his white, rolling eyes in a deprecatory smile.

Yes, what could worry her in all the world?—she who ought not to worry. He had an impulse then and there to begin a course of violent love. He remembered what he had thought of her when he was on the field; he remembered how they had grown up together; how he had taught her to sit a horse. He remembered how, before he had gone to the war, she had become a belle of that countryside. Yet, now that he was back at Westmore,—now, indeed, those phrases he might have worded seemed far-away and crude. She was not so much the girl he had fancied he was in love with as the simple, honest comrade of other days, —the girl who had not been behind in his rough sports; who could sit a horse,—he has recorded that he taught her,—and be as fearless as any one of us after the hounds; who could handle an oar or a sail; a jolly, Tomboy sort of a girl, who suddenly had settled down into the quieter ways of conscious maidenhood. Quieter, did I say? Was there ever so great a flirt as Sallie in those days? as many besides Kit could attest. So they walked on, leading the horses; and a hound ran out and recognized the returned Kit, and this brought the two back to other matters,—of the dogs and the horses, of what had happened at and about Westmore. And the girl was laughing, and Kit was answering her back, when suddenly Sallie sobered and turned to him.

"How, Kit, about the drinking?"

Now there had been a time when Kit had

been drinking too much, as was not an uncommon vice among gentlemen in those times. It's a rather easy matter to get to drinking too much, you know; and it so changes a man. Kit has ever held the theory that you owe it to your fellow-man to be agreeable; and, so, some drink is a blessing. It raises a man to the level of agreeability. But, then, I fear Kit had it in him to overstep the line. It was so easy a matter to get to a condition where it took ever more to reach that level.

"I have been rather careful about that," said Kit. "To be sure, you know, a man has to."

"And are the girls in New York so charming?" said Sallie.

"I think I've compared 'em all with one in Virginia," said our young gentleman, airily. (To this narrator, as he looks back on him, it was as if he were that young man's father; he can see his mistakes with a great pity, and envy, too. Oh, for the joy life sometimes gave in those days! Oh, for the old zest of pleasure and of tingling blood! The narrator feels, after all, that he has become a degenerate from that full-blooded, generous young captain he is commenting on of Mrs. Madison's jolly days,—days when formality and regard for old usages still obtained!)

"Kit, you've still a tongue for compliments. I have heard you paid Peggy Waters many when you made such furious love to her in Georgetown."

"Not I," said Kit.

"Well, I should like to know if it wasn't," Sallie cried, with a pout. "I know you better than you do yourself where a pretty face is concerned."

"Well, my lady, what of Lieutenant Wofington, the Englishman?"

"But I wasn't to blame because he admired me," said Sallie.

"And there's Sam Landers?"

"He is," said Sallie, "a very nice fellow."

"Oh, I dare say! I dare say!" said Kit, in a considerable rage.

"I tell you what I will agree to, Kit," Sallie said, at last. "I will say no more of Peggy——"

"If I'll say no more of the others; there are so many," said Kit, contemptuously.

"Well, if you talk in that way, Kit,—down, Jock!" to the hound,—"you needn't come over to-night. We didn't know you were back or else you would have been bidden."

"And now," said Kit, "there appears to be no chance in the world. I deliberately have closed the door."

Simon Wesley, lingering far behind, may have wondered or not. Simon was looking down at the Potomac, and now calling to Jock, who remembered him as he did his master.

"My uncle doubtless would be glad to see you," said Sallie, finally.

"And not you, Sallie?" Kit said. "I am only back for the day. I am on my way to New Orleans,—to report to Governor Claiborne,—to await General Jackson's orders about a company."

She suddenly faced him with a look almost of fright in her eyes.

"You are going to New Orleans,—New Orleans of all places?"

"Why not there as well as to another place?" Kit asked, wondering a bit, and with a sudden access of vanity.

"Oh, I don't know," said she, hesitatingly. "It is so far away. And, then, they say there'll be fighting."

"Do you care?" Kit asked, drawing nearer, but she pushed him back with a burst of laughter.

"Not a bit, you foolish boy,—not a bit, I assure you. You are wonderfully vain."

"Oh, am I?" Kit asked, with some chagrin. "I think I'll say good-by."

"How foolish our talk sounds! What's the use of a quarrel when at the best you are here only for a day?" said Sallie. "No, Kit, you must come over. I shall be sorry if you don't. As for New Orleans, it suggests something to me. They say it's a very fine city; and you'll find pleasure and gaming,—as much as you wish. And then there'll be some soldiering, too," she added. "Now I must go in; and we'll expect you in an hour."

The old house stood white and beckoning in its meadow as the two hesitated. Jock was now stretched out at his mistress's feet, her black tugging at the bridle in a thought of the stable.

"Sallie, dear," Kit began at last.

"Oh, bother!" she cried, and before he knew it she was in the saddle and up the path, her hat fallen back and a fine tangle of yellow hair swinging a mockery at him; and he mounted and rode back to Westmore, thinking that his talk with his little neighbor had not been exactly satisfactory. He was in a perplexity at himself; he had been at the point of asking her a very serious question, but she wouldn't listen.

"Where've you been?" asked the master of Westmore as his nephew returned.

"Over to the Maurices. I met Sallie on the road. I am invited there to-night."

"Humph!" said John Robe, pausing, and looking his nephew over. "I thought you were here to see me?"

"You wouldn't have me rude when I have known Sallie all my life?" Kit asked.

"Oh, no,—not rude. Only remember that it's bad blood,—bad blood."

"You always say that, sir," Kit put in. "They're held by others a very old family."

"They are," said old John Robe; "they are, to be sure. But it's her blood, you know. She's only half a Maurice."

"Hers?" said Kit, for he didn't know such a story. In that countryside, where gossip flew about swiftly enough, there never was a hint of such a complication. "Eh! what d'ye mean, uncle?" His blood suddenly was warm. He was angered at that uncle for the first time in many a year.

"Oh, it's nothing,—nothing!" John Robe hastened to cry out. "You know he and I are not very good friends."

Kit knew this very well. They had quarrelled and fought a duel years since over a lady who afterwards became Mrs. Maurice. (John Robe probably had lost in that skirmish, and he had remained a bachelor.) The lady in the case was dead these many years; the hope of the Maurice estate was in Sallie, the daughter of a certain ne'er-do-weel brother,—his probably was the bad blood of which nobody spoke openly. Kit knew these things, and knowing them he now sat down to pacify his uncle as best he might. And presently they were talking of other matters,—of the great Farewell Address they once had heard together, an account of which circumstance makes the opening of this narrative.

Kit can see this old gentleman now; very tall, broad-shouldered, with at his tongue's end reminiscences of all those distinguished Americans of our Revolutionary period, and, indeed, of France at that time. For, still a very young man, John Robe had been one of the commissioners to France. He had known Marie Antoinette in the heyday of her beauty, in the splendor of her position. He had been acquainted with those French gentlemen, whose names are now historical figures, who had ended in the great overthrow. The Marquis de la Fayette had been one of his good friends, and it's a matter of some pride with the Robes that when the marquis came to America Westmore was one of the houses he counted it a privilege to visit. But of all the history since, till English and French cruisers began to impress our seamen, and England counted us a country to be brought back to the colony,— all this had been of little moment to him, momentous though it had been. He had been content to lead the life of a Virginia country gentleman of that period, looking out more or less for his nephew's future. Kit had been at Yale College in Connecticut, and then he had taken the grand tour, as some Americans did. In those days he was the friend of a certain New York gentleman, since very distinguished in letters, a Mr. Washington Irving; and Mr. Irving has attested that there was no better, no finer type of the Virginia gentleman than John Robe. More than a mere country gentleman. Had he not been more or less distinguished in Congress during the Revolutionary period, a staunch adherent of our first great chief? Now, in his older days, he was filled with rare reminiscence of which no one could appreciate the fine flavor better than Mr. Irving. Or perhaps Kit may add to this statement of appreciation his nephew's, who hung on his lips with a certain interest that even Sir Walter Scott's famous novels were not able to arouse later.

Or may I not continue here some description of Westmore as it was in those days? Now the old house keeps its distinction as one of the great places in Virginia; but in those days of Kit's youth it had, as well as the surroundings, the gayety, now gone, the splendid ladies and gentlemen whom we now only read about. And many of them, the most interesting, too, never reached so far as the histories. Kit remembered particularly how he sat listening that evening, and the old servants, with certain deferential grins for the returned young master, passed in and out, till at last came the hour to pay that visit at the Maurices.

"Well, if you must leave me," said John Robe, rising laboriously, and calling to Alexander, better Alex, his man, who came in at the master's call.

"I'm not to be with you long," said John Robe. "And to-morrow you start."

"To-morrow I start."

"And yet you persist in going to the Maurices. Eh, a pretty face, a pretty ankle."

Kit did not gainsay that; for, indeed, why would he have cared to leave his uncle were it not as the master of Westmore stated? What other reasons were there, indeed? Yet, as in the moonshine he rode over to the Maurices, a certain remorse gripped his heart. Why should he be running away from that dear old uncle on this last night? And memories stirred him, as they will sometimes; regrets for what has been, which never may be again.

At his journey's end he was met by a little old man, who wore a wig, a certain parchment-like face, a manner interested and courtly, a carefulness in dress, a certain slyness in the eyes that Kit did not like.

"Sallie will be down directly," said Philip Maurice. "I hear you have distinguished yourself."

"Oh, I don't know," the captain replied. "It's easy to get notice in these times."

"Yes, of some sort or another," the host replied, "very easy. Oh, I hear you are going to New Orleans. Dan!"—and a negro servant appeared,—"a note I left on my desk.

"There's a man there of considerable importance,—a rich, influential man, though he has been branded a pirate. Hem! Mr. Christopher, this is a letter introducing you to Mr. Jean Lafitte, of New Orleans."

"I have heard the name," Kit answered. "Ah, yes, that man!"

"Oh, it won't hurt you; he's the most influential man in Louisiana, I tell you."

But Kit was thinking. He himself will tell you later what that name meant. What name, indeed, more influential? What name more significant for riches gained by illicit means? And yet Mr. Maurice doubtless was right about the usefulness of such a letter. Kit pocketed it with a bow. And just then the mistress of the house entered, very sweet and pretty in her simple gown.

But Kit was not to have her by himself. Sam Landers was expected. And how Sam Landers entered you may like to know; a rough, good-hearted, red-faced—for a hard-drinking—fellow; one of the richest proprietors in the State. And he was making love to Sallie? Kit had no more time to say what he might have wished to say.

Yet he bore away with him a picture of her as she stood against the light from the opened hall-door.

"I am sorry to have you go, Kit."

"Good-by, Sallie."

"You'll do your part?"

"Oh, I'll try," said he, pressing her hand. "Good-by, Sallie."

And he rode away to the wars again,—to those events which were to so change him; to the engrossing life outside, beyond that quiet rurality.

But it's well for a man to hold one girl superior to the others, particularly when she really is so. Such a devotion keeps one sometimes from those errors which leave moral scars.

And Kit rode away to the wars again, I have said. What those wars were,—what happened to him,—how strange things occurred to him,—are not all these things the subjects of this veracious history?

And, oh, the old days! And, oh, the joys of living when the old perplexities, the old defeats, the old victories held our hearts!

CHAPTER II

NEW ORLEANS

You doubtless know so well the situation in that year of 1814 that I need not recall the circumstances leading Captain Christopher Robe to Louisiana. We were then, after some years of tedious war, apparently as little near the end as at the beginning. To be sure, we had established our prestige as a sea-power of the first rank. But it makes Kit's heart sick now to recall all the governmental weaknesses,—delays, inappreciation of our lack of coast defences, or that military, not civil, training makes the captain,—all the follies committed in the name of the United Government. We had not been able to avoid the disgrace of the burning of our Capitol, nor the ravage of its neighborhood. Nor has there been more than hinted, in describing Kit's little visit to Westmore,

CHALMETTE 37

the condition of feeling, the consternation prevailing there.

Now the whole British armament on our coast was directed against far-away Louisiana, which we had bought so recently from Napoleon, and where there was among the French and the Spanish people small liking for the United States. The government sent down four troops of regulars, placed Commodore Patterson in command of the naval defences, and ordered out the State militia of about a thousand. Then they appointed General Andrew Jackson to command the Southwest. It had chanced that young Captain Robe had once served with General Jackson and had done a service which the general remembered. Kit always said that under the general's exterior he saw those remarkable abilities which made him one of the most efficient generals, and later, for all his peculiarities, one of the greatest Presidents of the United States. What that particular service was need not be recounted here. A man may not care to repeat vainly what is out of the course of the particular story he is telling. But when Captain Robe applied for service in Louisiana, his imagination having been fired by the situation there, General Jackson himself seconded the proposition, and so it chanced that he was ordered to report at New Orleans to wait further advices.

Robe has often related how splendid the city seemed after his long journey thither; how the strange street crowds, so contrasted in color and tongues, affected him; how he found a gayety, a luxury, an ease of manner, that no part of America afforded the like. He fell easily into the ways of that generous hospitality. For even in the day of fear the creoles did not forget that life is charming, that one should be gay. He attended many balls and functions, for he had many invitations, having been well introduced. He listened to the talk in coffee-houses, to reports that many seemed to wish to believe that the red and black Spanish flag would soon again float over the devoted town.

This General Jackson couldn't defend them, they said; bah! a rough frontier fighter against the Peninsular veterans, against the fleet that had fought under Nelson. 'Twas ridiculous in the extreme. And there would follow ejaculations and a rush of language that Kit couldn't understand. For though our young captain had a fair schooling in Latin, he hardly knew Spanish from French, and so you will find in this account naught but plain English. And what is more, they went on, these English have the Indians, and, —horror of horrors!—they will liberate the slaves. And then they would lean forward and tell in English, for our young captain's benefit, fearsome tales of the massacres in San Domingo, where the slaves had risen against their masters. Many a New Orleans family came from San Domingo, and the stories of that horrid affair,—of the atrocities committed, of the narrow escapes,—were told over again and again. British regulars were at Pensacola. British ships were in the Gulf. Ah, what would happen to this New Orleans, that had passed from Spaniard to Frenchman, from Frenchman to Yankee!

Kit being but a poor writer, being eager

to get to his own adventures, must despair of describing all he saw in that interesting city in those exciting days; where fear neither stopped the theatres nor the active challenge of black eyes, to some of whose owners he proceeded to make himself agreeable. That he succeeded it is not for himself to say.

Of course, to resume his narrative, he reported, and then delivered some despatches he was bearer of to that distinguished Governor Claiborne, one of the great American names. At Governor Claiborne's he met a certain old acquaintance, a Dennis Cafferty, whom he had known in New Haven. Dennis was a calm, matter-of-fact person; very honest and strong in every way, who had a certain scorn for this pleasure-loving city. The two friends talked it over many times, Kit defending his point of view, but Dennis came from a family of North of Ireland Presbyterians and stood by his own.

"Look, Kit, you'll be going about too much," he said. "It's easy to fall here. Yes, easy enough, I know. And you'll end in a duel, I tell ye."

Kit only laughed at this, and, being a lover of pleasure and having been brought up to certain easy-going Virginian traditions, he found a rather more congenial companion in a certain young gentleman,—a Raoul Deschamps,—whom he met at Mrs. Claiborne's, herself a very charming lady. I am not sure that Kit liked this tall, thin, black-eyed Deschamps so well at first, but they ended by discovering certain tastes in common. Kit was not averse to a bit of gaming. You could have that in New Orleans. He was not opposed to attending those wonderful public balls, and Deschamps opened the way.

"You'd reconcile us to Americans, you Virginians," Deschamps said one day after the theatre. New Orleans loved the play then as well as now.

"I seem to be very well acquainted now," said Kit. "But I haven't presented one of my letters to your great pirate, Lafitte."

"Ah, that's wrong," said Deschamps, smiling, and showing his fine white teeth; "Jean Lafitte is one of the greatest financiers in the world. Why, two-thirds of us in New Orleans owe whatever we have to the trade he has made possible."

"Governor Claiborne has launched enough proclamations against him. General Jackson has called him a 'hellish bandit,'" quoth Robe.

"Ugh," said Deschamps. "Don't you know, my Kit, that an opinion is just the color of a man's interest. You say you have a letter for him. Let me see it, pray."

And Kit handed him the letter from Mr. Maurice to Jean Lafitte:

"My dear Sir,—This will introduce to your good favor Mr. Christopher Robe, of the army, who is a neighbor of ours and heir of the Westmore estates, of which you know.

"Hoping that you may be well and that your affairs may be as usually prosperous,
 "I am
  "Yours faithfully,
   "Philip Maurice."

As Deschamps read it he looked up quickly. "I will take you around there now."

"Where?" asked Kit, wondering; "he's outlawed."

"What's the difference? The government owes too much to him. He's safe enough."

"But the other brother, Pierre Lafitte, is in prison without bail."

"What's the difference?" Raoul Deschamps said again. "I know he's here. Don't disregard such an invitation. He's a man to know,—the most powerful in New Orleans,—a most agreeable gentleman."

"You remember I am an officer of the United States," Kit said, still hesitating.

"I don't see that you commit yourself by so simple an affair as a visit," said the other.

"But I may feel bound to report that I have seen him."

"They know that well enough, but they don't dare to touch him. You will see a man who has made the trade of the Mississippi Valley."

"Well," said Kit, "it's good of you, and, of course, I shall be delighted."

And they went out into the warm night,

where the varied crowd was still pushing, laughing, jesting, with now and then a more serious tone; such a wonderful crowd as you cannot see of these days: negro women with bright Madras handkerchiefs; a finely-dressed gentleman contrasted with a rough sailor, or a trapper, gaunt, in his rough hunting clothes. For New Orleans was not yet asleep, as Kit knew of other nights like this. He had found an elegance, an extravagance he never had before fancied, reaching down into the lower classes. And this night there had been many festivities, three balls, one of the negroes, another of the quadroons, and another of the gentle folk, which the friends had not attended.

As they passed on they came across a little party preceded by three sturdy blacks, whose swinging lanterns showed two ladies following, with, at their heels, two chattering maids dangling their mistresses' slippers. Kit caught a glimpse of a pretty ankle, of dark, charming eyes, of a low, narrow brow framed by black hair, of a thin, pale face, and a little mouth with enticing lips, wondrous red against the pale face; the figure rather tall and full.

How in some first impressions, even by a swinging lantern, do some faces leave themselves fixed in your memory, never to be entirely obliterated from that tablet! You may pass many thousands a day, and but one, for some strange reason of personality, is recorded clearly by your eyes.

Deschamps stopped now on the way to that late visit. He was bowing in the most stately manner possible,—bending low; the fashion has gone out now with many good old fashions; manners began to deteriorate in the degree that formality in dress was given up, with gentlemen's silk stockings and shoes with silver and gold buckles.

The blacks stopped as if by magic. The elder lady greeted Kit's friend very finely, with a smile through her rouge. She was rather old, Kit fancied, and highly colored in complexion, and gowned like a bird of paradise. Her voice came out thin and a bit cracked, in French. In the background the younger lady sent Kit a coquettish smile.

Deschamps turned.

"Madame de Renier, Captain Christopher Robe, the Virginia Robes, and Mademoiselle Marie de Renier."

Madame bowed graciously, and said in very good English that, indeed, she was glad to meet one of Mr. Deschamps's friends, particularly when he was a Virginia Robe. (Now I wonder if she really ever had heard the name before.) Mademoiselle inclined her pretty, bird-like head and softly giggled. It was, I assure you, a most delightful giggle, like a maiden's light heart bubbling over, and Kit found his mind well fixed on the owner of it. (And all this proves that what Sallie had said about him may have been right. Had she known him better than he knew himself?) Kit thought, at any rate, that Mademoiselle de Renier was a very enticing person. Madame in the mean time was assuring Mr. Deschamps that she would be delighted to have him bring his friend; that they would like to have them both down next week for two days on the plantation.

She turned with a bow, ordering her servants on. Mademoiselle looked back roguishly over her shoulder. And they went on to the accompaniment of swinging lanterns.

"A deucedly pretty girl," said Kit.

"Many have thought so much," Mr. Raoul assented. "We'll see more of her. Ah, how she dances! What eyes she has!"

"They were interesting," Kit agreed.

"Now we are to Mr. Lafitte's," said Deschamps.

Robe will not attempt to describe where the house of that important person—that rascal or patriot—happened to be. They had a way of numbering streets very badly, or not at all, in New Orleans of those days, and it's sufficient to say that they came to a dwelling of some pretension. Nor was there much caution in admitting them, though there might be a price on the owner's head. The interior was surprising in the luxury of its appointments, though Deschamps whispered to Kit that he should see the plantation at the Grande Terre on the Bay of Barataria.

Now, while Kit waits to see this man to whom he bore the letter,—wondering what the great manager of the Barataria enterprise could be like; this pirate and outlaw, who yet was declared a polished gentleman,— let us pause to describe who he was.

Do you remember the tales of pirates who infested the Gulf; all those bloody events that boys like to listen to with wide eyes? Well, a time came when his British Majesty frightened them from their quondam resorts, and they found in the innumerable winding interways between the mouth of the Mississippi and the Bayou La Fourche a locality where their ships could slip in and out. Protected by the narrow strip of land, the Grand Terre, was the Bay of Barataria. Here this gentry made a settlement, a refuge, a home, a trading-post. The Mississippi could distribute their wares over a continent. Not far away was the city, made up of a mixed population from the four corners of the earth, not too anxious to inquire into *meum* and *tuum*.

In those days two shrewd brothers, Jean

and Pierre Lafitte, came from Bayonne to better their fortunes. From blacksmiths, having the sense of trade, they became proprietors, and from disposing of a cargo for some individual owner, they became the bankers and agents of them all, and directly the managers of the commercial community which grew up around Baratarian Bay,—Barataria.

And how was that merchandise acquired? Much on the high seas, much from looted merchantmen; much, indeed, bought somewhere legitimately, perhaps for the proper coupled with the less considerable profit of paying no duties. There were few families in New Orleans not in some way dependent on that trade, whatever its source,—in piracy or in smuggling; in any view it was lawless enough. No question was made that much, as I have said, was from pirates' spoils, even if the Baratarians declared that they were very proper privateers, with papers from the newly-revolted Spanish colonies privileging them to prey on Spanish commerce. 'Twas a generally-accepted fact that they made no particular distinction about the nationality of the vessel could they get it and scuttle it and leave no soul to tell the story. In Kit's boyhood those who sailed the Gulf ran the continual risk of pirates, and we in these days can hardly understand how that part of the world has changed. We cannot fancy the romance, the terror of it then.

The power and wealth of Barataria became so prodigious that in 1813, the preceding year, Governor Claiborne issued a proclamation denouncing it all. But who minded that? Who gave so lavishly to charity as the two Lafittes? And they walked the streets with their heads high, the very pictures of success. And the ships still brought in wines, silks, slaves, everything, which were as openly auctioned as ever. A British sloop-of-war tried its hand at two of the Baratarian vessels and was vigorously driven away. The Baratarians were prepared to fight, like an independent nationality, as, indeed, made up of all nations, they nearly were. A revenue collector and one of his men were killed. When the governor asked

CHALMETTE 51

the Legislature for a force to clear out this nest of illicit trade and piracy, the legislators remembered—scandal ran—their master. And now, when Kit paid his visit, the two leaders, Jean and Pierre Lafitte, were criminally indicted,—Pierre in the calaboose without bail, and Jean somewhere, a fugitive. A fugitive, did I say? It appeared that this Jean was actually in New Orleans, and here was our captain of the army paying him a visit. The trial was even then going on. The clever Jean had employed celebrated counsel, one no less than the district attorney, who resigned his position of public prosecutor for a twenty-thousand-dollar fee. Pirates, my dear Louisianians! These men be patriots, your best citizens, who are building the commercial prestige and greatness of your State.

Kit, you may be sure, knew these stories, and many more that I have not put down here, and he had hesitated when Mr. Maurice had given him the letter. But now Raoul Deschamps had said that Mr. Jean Lafitte would be in, like any ordinary citizen; and he was actually awaiting him at this late hour of the evening. Deschamps had sent up his name and Kit's letter, and the servant, a suave mulatto, brought back word that his master would see the gentlemen. There was no attempt at evasion.

What had Kit expected to see in this formidable person? There entered shortly a black-haired, black-eyed man,—what penetrating, fine, black eyes!—fair-complexioned, splendid-mannered, and attired like any gentleman of New Orleans back from some occasion. His voice was gentle and persuasive.

Yes, he had known Mr. Maurice in other days, and he was glad to know any one of Mr. Maurice's friends, particularly when he chanced to be a member of the army which was to defend New Orleans from the enemy. Possibly Kit stared. Was this the outlaw,— this proper gentleman, voicing fine, patriotic phrases?

"I want to know you all," he went on to the young Virginian. "I want you to be on my side as opposed to the governor's,—for, hem! the governor is mistaken in some things."

Kit thought he must be. His own reserve thawed. This winning gentleman carried him outside of himself; and Raoul Deschamps sat in the corner and smiled.

"The governor must know that I can help him in this crisis,—that I have armed men to put in the field," our gentleman went on almost nonchalantly.

But at the moment there came a great pounding and rattling. The mulatto servant rushed in, whispering something to his master, whose voice came out rather fiercely:

"They have dared!"

A keen, angry light was in his eyes.

"They have dared!" said Raoul, rising; and then he said something rapidly in French. The host nodded, muttered a few words low to Raoul, and then turned to Kit without any change of manner.

"I regret that our first interview should be so interrupted, Mr. Robe," and he extended his hand and was gone,—calm, strong, masterful.

"He is safe enough," said Deschamps then.

"You mean they are here to arrest him?" Captain Robe asked.

"They can't. He has only to step out of a door that opens into the adjoining house,—a door they don't know about,—and he is among the French. Is there a creole who would betray Jean Lafitte? He was here to see his attorney."

The knocking had stopped; there was the clatter of feet outside. Voices sounded. Presently there entered Kit's friend, Dennis Cafferty, of the militia, with behind him John Turnbull, a Boston man, on the governor's staff.

Cafferty paused in some amazement at his friend.

"He is not here?" he asked.

"No, you can't find him," Raoul Deschamps said. "I refer you to Mr. Grymes, his lawyer."

"I think you are right," the other said; "a foolish undertaking. The sheriff wouldn't do it. The governor thought he would try himself to entrap his old foe."

"Well, I am sorry," Deschamps laughed. "We will go with you if you don't mind."

Outside Cafferty took Kit by the arm.

"It's indiscreet of you to stand with their party. The fall of Barataria will make some pretty scandals in New Orleans. Remember, your orders may come any time. This may ruin you with General Jackson."

"Oh, I can care for myself," the Virginian retorted with some spirit. "But you are a good fellow, Dennis," he added.

"You go about too much; you play too much; you care too much for pleasure," his friend retorted.

"Oh, I'll not lose my temper with you. We Robes have always gone our own ways, —such as they are. And so long as two-thirds of New Orleans are on the side of the Lafittes, I don't see what difference this can make to me. But, Dennis, be a good fellow; I'm curious. What can they want of me?"

"Pooh!" said Dennis, "it's their policy to stand well with every man, not knowing when they may wish to use him. As for you, you may influence your uncle's opinion, and your uncle stands well with Congress."

"I say," Raoul cried out here, "you failed!"

They were walking in the dim streets with a dozen men of the governor's posse. If the governor were disregarding the municipal authorities, it wouldn't matter,—if he could get Jean Lafitte lodged with his brother Pierre in the calaboose.

"Yes, we've failed in several things. Among others, Pierre Lafitte is no longer in jail."

"Escaped!" Raoul cried in affected surprise; for Kit saw that he had known.

"Yes," said Cafferty, sullenly. "Are you coming with Turnbull and me, Kit?"

No, Kit had an engagement with Mr. Deschamps; and he and Mr. D. went laughing away arm in arm. Of course, these violations of the law were very serious. But why should you have a wry face and manners towards those whose hospitality is giving you an agreeable time? When it came to the point of the United States going down to clear out this Barataria, if Kit had an appointment there, he would go down there cheerfully. But he had not been bred in the school of New England prejudice of Turnbull and the Irish-Scot's son. He was a Virginian, with a Virginian's liberal views on certain matters.

And where did they go? I will not tell you all the places they went to that night. They were, I declare, no worse than most of us; at least, Kit was not. They found themselves at last over the cards among a crowd of gentlemen, among whom was Mr. Grymes, the lawyer, who told them that he and Mr. Livingston certainly would gain the cases of the Lafittes, at which a cheer ran up.

"But Jean takes a risk in coming up here?" one asked.

"Did he ever refuse a risk?" another answered. "It's not fear of New Orleans, but his duty in Barataria, which keeps him there."

"Jean Lafitte fear the State government! Why, my friends, he controls that government."

As for Kit, I am afraid he lost more than he ought. I am afraid that Simon Wesley—bless his honest, white soul in a black body!—put his master to bed tipsy.

At least, late the next morning Kit awoke with an aching head. And then he fell to thinking of Sallie back there in Virginia. He remembered all he had said, and, if not actually said, implied to her. He felt rather miserable and mean-spirited. But after he had eaten he began to feel better. Memory of Sallie was chased out of his mind, to be replaced by the dark-eyed girl whom he had seen in the flaring lantern-light. He repeated the name, Marie de Renier; and then he went out to keep an appointment with Raoul. His orders would come soon enough. He would make the most of the pleasures of the gay city.

And the sun was shining; and New Orleans was chattering and smiling.

CHAPTER III

MADEMOISELLE DE RENIER

Mademoiselle de Renier and Robe slipped easily into acquaintanceship. She had a way, inherited from a long line of charming women, of holding men's attention. And, indeed, there was in Kit's time few more entertaining young ladies; I declare, women are not what they were in his youth, or men either. 'Tis the fashion to say that you are finer, better now. Well, it may be. Robe does not agree with you. And as for New Orleans, 'twas a Paris transplanted. The New Orleans of the early part of the century was a surprise, indeed, with its delightful social sophistication.

I have left Robe in a way that made his friends, Dennis Cafferty and John Turnbull, shake their heads. He was going to the dogs; he was too often at the gaming-tables; you could see him now and then with cheeks flushed, his steps a bit unsteady. I am sure it was a case deplorable enough. But it's an ordeal that most of us pass through sooner or later. Possibly we should be purer of heart if we didn't; but 'tis the way of life; and generous, honest souls are caught in this net of pleasure, to be made perhaps brutal and selfish. 'Tis occurring every day, and it will to the world's end. You can't legislate it or preach it out; every man must solve his own problems in his own way. And if the morality were easy in New Orleans then, it was easy in London and in Paris in all conscience. Here, in a land of sunshine and nature's glory, was the old world itself, with little of that hard fight with primeval conditions which made the intrepid strength of New England, the Middle States, and the West. Yet wait for this history's course; you will find as strong and fine a fight,—involving the greatest self-sacrifice,—you will listen to a victory as great, I think, as any Homer ever sang. But here I am anticipating, and forgetting that this story is mine only so far as Kit's fortunes were involved with it.

CHALMETTE

You may imagine him very much with the De Reniers, and Mademoiselle bore out the first impression he had of her. She had all the piquancies, the little graces, which may entice a man. She inherited them, indeed. Madame herself was of a very good family, which that atrocious Revolution had brought to New Orleans. Madame in her day had her score of suitors, though you might not always suspect it when you saw her in the morning, as Kit did. He passed several days on the De Renier plantation. He saw a great deal of Mademoiselle with an ever-increasing admiration. The one trouble was that there were too many suitors. Among these was a certain Louis Ronald, a little, agile man of great estate, a celebrated swordsman. At thirty he was said to have killed three men. Our Virginian took a dislike to him from the first; it was as instinctive as his liking for Mademoiselle.

And she smiled and encouraged them all. Was there ever such a capricious little flirt? Was there ever, to be truthful, in the end a more devoted wife? Those flirtatious damsels sometimes have the surest faith. But Mademoiselle passed through many experiences before she reached that point.

"How do you like us down here?" she asked one day, turning her pleading eyes on the Virginian. They were alone for a moment in a delicious glade. You might have fancied a thousand little loves flitting about in the shrubbery.

"How do I like you?" said Kit. "I love you." And he tried to take her hand.

"Oh, fie, Captain Robe," said she, as demure a damsel as you could wish. "That means nothing,—or everything."

"Or everything," Kit repeated. And just then Monsieur Ronald appeared.

"Is Monsieur learning French?" he asked, with a meaning smile.

Kit bridled a bit. It was his one chagrin that he didn't know French, and he never had time to learn it. You lost so much by not knowing the tongue in New Orleans.

"Eh, how's the army?" said Ronald affably. Mademoiselle was laughing.

CHALMETTE 63

"I am still waiting my orders," said Kit, rather stiffly.

"They say they intend attacking Mobile."

"Did you ever hear of a Lieutenant Beaumont on one of their ships, the 'Pensacola'?" said Mademoiselle.

"Why," said Ronald, for he was not long back from England, "he's to marry Lady Kitty Berford. I know him well."

Now it was a mystery to Kit why Ronald had been in England. He always suspected the worst of the man. But Raoul Deschamps told him later that Ronald's mother was an Englishwoman.

"How did you know this English officer, Mademoiselle Marie?" he asked.

Mademoiselle sat very still, her face pale and agitated. And Kit wondered why. But Monsieur Ronald took up the conversation.

"Everybody comes to New Orleans, Mr. Robe,—sooner or later,—even your good self."

"Yes, I dare say," Kit said, absently.

"Why, we had here in '98,—the princes themselves running from the guillotine,—

the Dukes d'Orleans, de Montpensier, the Comte de Beaujolais. The way we knew this Mr. Beaumont was that an English frigate, after chasing pirates, put in here a year before the war. He was very nice, Mademoiselle thought."

"I never liked him," Mademoiselle retorted, a little flush mounting her pale cheeks.

"Speaking of pirates," Monsieur Ronald went on, "Mr. Grymes has won his case."

"For the Lafittes," said Mademoiselle, turning. "They give so much for the public balls."

"He is going to a banquet at Barataria." Ronald went on.

"That exonerates them," said Kit, rising, for he found three a crowd that moment.

"You are not going?" Mademoiselle expostulated, looking up to him.

But he was. And he bowed stiffly. The rest of that visit he rather avoided her. If he had known, those were the very best tactics to have adopted. Mademoiselle had a certain common feminine weakness of caring most for those men who avoided her.

CHAPTER IV

THE LETTER

One day Mr. Grymes came back with the most wonderful stories of the hospitality he had received at the hands of the Lafittes at Barataria

" Pirates!" quoth he; "splendid gentlemen."

" What has become of your friend Robe?" he asked of Raoul Deschamps. "Doesn't that fellow play too much?"

"Oh, pooh," said Mr. Deschamps; "he's rich."

I must state here that gossip has it,—I don't vouch for the truth of any gossip,—that Mr Grymes had received his twenty thousand dollars fee, but on his return toward the city had stopped at several plantations where a quiet little rubber couldn't be refused, and when he reached the city not a penny was left of that fee. Well, Robe has seen many persons turn moralists after certain unfortunate experiences. His friends, Cafferty and Turnbull, might shake their heads, but then it was a tradition that all Southerners were naturally " devils of fellows."

But, now as he looks back at it all, Robe must confess that he was taking rather a lively pace. The drafts from New Orleans on Mr. Robe's banker in Baltimore were frequent and thick. As for the young gentlemen of New Orleans, they seemed to find in him one after their own taste, and, indeed, Mademoiselle de Renier was strongly inclined to encourage him, for he began to see that a certain disdain smooths the way to a woman's fancy.

So there came a gladsome morning when he awoke with a consciousness of jingling coin in his pocket. His head, too, was wondrous clear, considering the fact that he had been out rather late. And, as on another morning, he went out to the De Reniers', and they were alone for some moments.

"Ah," said Mademoiselle, with a sigh, " there are so many pretty girls in New Orleans."

"Do you remember what I told you once?" he asked.

"Yes," said she, timidly, and he leaned over and kissed her, and as he did he had suddenly a vision of Sallie Maurice. He could see Sallie's eyes in Mademoiselle's, could hear her voice, so that Mademoiselle suddenly drew back. But Robe knew what he had done, and he said again the words with a certain cold formality. He would act it out to the end, he said to himself, with self-pity. Yet what was his acting? Tears were in her eyes, and then, though he called after her, she was gone from the room. And Kit was like a man who has recovered from a long delirium. He sent word for Mademoiselle. She begged to be excused. Kit went out into the sunshine of the street and then back to his lodgings, where he wrote two notes,—one couched in very formal terms to Madame de Renier, asking for her daughter's hand and stating what his prospects were; and in the other he made again his declaration, and, calling Simon Wesley, he ordered him to get a bunch of roses and violets and to present them to Mademoiselle with her note. Simon grinned and went out. He, too, was having rather a pleasant time in New Orleans, though Northern darkies were not much esteemed by their creole fellows.

Kit sat very still, looking out of the window, but only seeing the face which had interrupted his love-making. Suddenly he knew himself; he knew it was the Virginia girl, not Mademoiselle.

Now you will say he should have known from the first that he was, indeed, a very fickle fellow. Well, while he is a hero of mine, I can't defend him. He was ever filled with all the human weaknesses and ficklenesses.

Now, as he sat there, he noticed on the table a letter addressed to him. Picking it up, he stared in wonder. It was Sallie's hand and Sallie's seal. He tore it open and read:

"Dear Kit,—I know all about you. Wasn't I right that day at Westmore? What if I had believed you? But I didn't.
"S. M."

That was all. If he had been in a calmer mood he might have been a little vain over Sallie's haste to explain that she didn't care; that he needn't deceive himself. But I am not sure that would have been a reason for vanity. It's possible for a woman to write such a note without caring at all for a man, that's certain.

But how did she know? New Orleans was so far away from Virginia. He had been there only three weeks. Or was she referring to some other vagary of his? He couldn't remember one that would call out her letter. Could she be in New Orleans? He remembered Philip Maurice's letter to Jean Lafitte. He must know, and he called for a servant of the house.

"How did this letter get here?" he asked.

"A half hour ago, sir; from the convent."

Without waiting to consider the situation further, he went out hastily. What did that mean?—the convent of the Ursulines.

I can see him now, as if he were another, as he walked through those streets and stopped at last before that famous building where for ninety years the sisters of Saint Ursula did their sweet, good work. He hesitated for a moment, looking at the stout brick walls. Was she indeed there? And what had brought her to New Orleans? He would ask; he would know. And he gently raised the knocker above the cross. As the porter looked out through the grated opening he asked if a Miss Maurice might be lodged there, and he showed the letter and explained his mission. At last there came word that Sister Madeleine would see him, and presently he was before a woman who must have been very beautiful in her time. Now her face had that holy air which the frame gives it, a reminiscence of sorrow which had added to the delicate refinement.

"Yes, Monsieur," she began; then, turning to English, "the letter was sent you from here."

"And is she here?"

"No, sir."

"Has she been?"

"Yes."

"Where can I find her?"

"Oh, I cannot tell you that, believe me, sir."

And suddenly she said:

"You have a good face,—a face that will be strong some day."

"Thank you, mother," Kit said, bowing humbly; and as he turned away he carried with him a picture of her calm, heavenly face. He seemed to be called back to his better self all at once.

And she had been there? He remembered that the Maurices were Romanists; he remembered how she had changed color when he had said he was on his way to Louisiana. And then he thought again of the letter to Jean Lafitte. Could that explain it all? She knew of his attentions to Marie de Renier. Ah, yes, it was now a betrothal. He walked more briskly to get the answer Simon might have brought. Simon was there; but it was a verbal message,—" Mademoiselle de Renier wishes to see Mr. Robe in person."

Mademoiselle was smiling as he entered; but the first words she uttered were,—

"I have torn up that note of yours,—and Madame's, ma mere's, too. She didn't see it."

"I meant it," he began.

"Why, you didn't at all. If you did you must be prepared to die of a broken heart,—for———"

"Why?" he asked.

"Do you know that story Louis Ronald told,—of a Lieutenant Beaumont?" Her voice rose to a certain tragic intensity. "I loved—I love—that man. I hate her———"

And Kit remembered that Ronald had said this English lieutenant was betrothed.

"As for you, dear Mr. Robe, I led you on. I liked you; I like you; but love!—it was between us a play; and it has ended in a jolly friendship."

And they shook hands and laughed, indeed, the best of friends; for he knew she was speaking the truth, and she understood him. She had angled for him and caught him,—which satisfied her coquetry; and now she was pleased to let him go. She confided in him a bit more about Beaumont, to which

CHALMETTE

he listened, while she ended, denying her words with a little stamp of the foot,—of course, she wasn't in earnest about that either. Was she trying to gain Robe back by naming a rival?

That evening Captain Robe received an order to accompany, by Governor Claiborne's request, Captain Cafferty, of the State militia, to examine into the pirates' retreat at Barataria, and to report to General Jackson at Mobile, where he had been making the defence of Fort Bowyer. The general knew the quality of Captain Robe's observation on a former occasion.

Kit remembers a proclamation of the general that was about the city the next day:

> "The base, perfidious Britons have attempted to invade your country. They had the temerity to attack Fort Bowyer with their incongruous horde of Indians, negroes, and assassins; they seem to have forgotten that this fort was defended by freemen."

Reading his instruction, and listening to its interpretation from the military commandant of New Orleans, Captain Robe felt very glad that now he had some plain duty. Nor did the fact that he had met Jean Lafitte through the introduction of the Maurices lessen his zest.

CHAPTER V

THE PIRATES OF BARATARIA

Not a soul was supposed to know of this expedition, but Robe doubts not in the least that the astute Lafitte was from the first aware of its every detail. He himself saw Raoul Deschamps, of course, without hinting of it, and he made a visit on Mademoiselle, who was very light and gracious and did not once suspect that he was going away. Kit may have wondered what the Virginia young lady would have said to these continual visits. But really he couldn't avoid being polite to Mademoiselle after he had made himself such a fool about her. And then there came the further details of the expedition. Captain Robe made several suggestions, which were accepted as valuable. They must see Jean Lafitte himself, General Jackson had said; they must look over Barataria as carefully as their chance would permit. Jean Lafitte was not inclined to come to New Orleans at that time; and his brother Pierre was not a substitute for Jean, who controlled the fighting Baratarians. Jean was to be dealt with directly. Major Cafferty was to represent the State, and Captain Robe General Jackson himself. They took with them six men,— seven, indeed, including Simon Wesley, who was an active fellow.

And at dawn one September morning they put out for Barataria.

As their sloop went down the river—in that scene where nature had been so lavish in colors, in delicious beauty—the languor of the day fell over them; all quite astonishing to the Virginian, who had not yet become too familiar with that charming scenery. He and Cafferty were now on good terms, and Dennis told over again how he had come to New Orleans and succeeded beyond his expectation. Neither of the two had much complaint to make of success, and Robe could tell a pretty story of what he had done at Lundy's Lane,—by the purest chance, he must add in strict frankness.

They stopped for lunch at a plantation, whose owner was said not to be in the Baratarian interest. While this gentleman, a Mr. Brownell—married into a creole family—talked, Kit went outside in the hot sunshine. His few weeks of leisure in New Orleans seemed far away, and only one thing piqued, —Sallie Maurice's presence in New Orleans, the mystery Sister Madeleine did not choose to explain, or, perhaps, could not in duty to herself.

" Ah, Captain Robe, how does it chance that you are as far down as here?" came a sarcastic voice, and he saw Louis Ronald.

" How do ye do?" said Kit, coldly, ignoring the question. " What a charming day !"

" I fancy that Major Cafferty has some mission of importance," Ronald went on. " You are pointed towards Barataria. Possibly there's been a report of a new cargo of blacks."

" Possibly," said Robe. " You are a friend of Mr. Brownell?"

" Mr. Brownell is one of the most popular Americans in Louisiana," Ronald said, easily.

"You know Americans are not altogether so. They are still much foreigners to us with French prejudices. You can't uproot in a generation a feeling born in the blood. And then the Spanish annexation feeling is very strong."

"The British count on that, and the Baratarians, I believe," said Robe, slowly. "It appears to have been a good move to try to stir up the race feeling. I can't believe they will be barbarians enough to free the slaves——"

"All kinds of reports are rife," said Ronald, easily. "But I think General Jackson has his hands full."

Robe made no reply to this, but afterwards, when they were started again, he told Cafferty the talk word for word. (At luncheon Mr. Brownell had accounted for Ronald's presence by stating that he had the adjoining plantation.)

"He is an agent of the Lafittes," Cafferty said; "two-thirds of the Louisianians are, for that matter. Then there's another party, made up of Northerners, who would like to loot Barataria; there are so many tales of untold treasures hidden there. Was ever a place where so many adventurers were gathered! But as for Ronald,—eh, he's a dangerous fellow. You may believe we're expected on the Bay of Barataria."

"Could he get a word there before us?"

"Humph!" Cafferty retorted, "in this labyrinth of water-ways nothing could be easier. But they probably knew it from New Orleans the moment the expedition was decided on. Ours a useless sort of enterprise, too. Those men would dare anything. But last year, you know, a revenue officer and two of his men were killed and the rest held prisoners. To be sure, our visit is amicable enough."

As they went on Dennis told many stories of Captain's Dominique You and Robert de Bertrand, of whom Robe was to know much.

They had reached a point in their course where the glimmer of the bay was sparkling blue through the opening of a lagoon, when a voice sang out, "Surrender!" and instantly a dozen boats pushed out from the banks filled with wild, picturesque fellows bearing levelled muskets and bare cutlasses.

"Not a movement," Dennis sang out to his men in French and English. "There are two score of them."

The captain of the sloop obeyed by bringing it to.

"We have a mission for Mr. Lafitte," Cafferty shouted.

The others did not answer, but came up laughing and shouting threats in three tongues and piling over the side.

"I tell you we are not here for the revenues," Cafferty cried in French.

"My dear captain," said the leader, a little, swarthy fellow, "it makes no difference. We must take possession."

"You'll suffer for this," Cafferty said. "Your nest will be cleared out."

"Submit, my dear Monsieur," the leader went on with a certain mockery of urbanity. "What else can you do? And then let them come down on us. They have been talking of it so long."

Robe was fidgeting, for he was thinking

of drawing his pistols and making a fight for it; but then his good sense returned. They could but submit meekly.

"That's all, Cafferty," he said; "our mission will protect us."

And he looked out at the fierce crew that had captured them, jabbering, as I say, in three tongues, and I know not how many dialects, looking for all the world like figures in some romantic play, though, to be sure, in plays actors of rough parts are too well clad. And behind all was the luxuriant foliage, the gleaming sun, the shining waters.

"Your weapons, Messieurs," said the leader, again, bowing politely; "now we must bind you."

"Does Mr. Lafitte or Captain Dominique You or Captain de Bertrand know of this?" Cafferty asked.

"Who knows?" laughed the leader. "It may be the order of the Republic of Cartha-gena. As for the captains, they may be sailing the seas over. Eh, Cafferty," for he seemed to know Kit's friend.

"Eh, Pierre La Roux, you keep on your

same high-handed course. But there'll be an end to it, my friend, an end to it," Cafferty cried, his gray eyes flashing, his red hair shaking like a lion's shaggy mane, for his cap had fallen. The captain of the sloop and the escort seemed ready to resist against the numbers of the assailants. But Robe put his hand on his friend's shoulder.

"Don't be a fool, Dennis. You know I'm no coward, but a fool is as bad as one."

"You're right, man," said Dennis, suddenly calm. "Give up your arms, fellows. We'll have to depend on Mr. Lafitte's mercy."

"Mr. Lafitte doesn't know of this," La Roux said with his smile; he seemed to be ever smiling.

"I think you lie," Dennis retorted.

"Well, well, what's a lie, Cafferty?" La Roux said, shrugging his shoulders. "I have said it. You may believe me or no, as it pleases you."

He turned, giving an order in French and repeating it in Spanish, for Captain Robe had begun to distinguish between the two tongues, and, indeed, to gather a smattering of the former. As the order passed, La Roux turned to the prisoners:

"You must be blindfolded, my friends, and your hands tied behind you."

"Well, my friend," Captain Robe said at this, "we'll submit; I'll speak for Major Cafferty. But let your leader know that I come from General Jackson, and that he will do well to hear me."

"Humph," said La Roux, viciously, and then more quietly and with a return of that mocking politeness, "I'm the leader here."

"As you spoke of your lie, 'I have said it,'" Captain Robe said. "The privateers of Carthagena, if that's what you call yourselves, must respect the condition of envoys."

"Well-a-day, sir," said La Roux, "we'll consider that afterwards."

Cafferty stood mute, lest he again should break into anger.

The men's hands were bound behind them and then they were blindfolded. Simon Wesley looked pleadingly at his master, his teeth chattering. He expected nothing less than to be shot.

"Trust to me, Simon," said his master with a nonchalance he himself didn't feel. Cafferty edged to him.

"My belief is," he said in a low voice, "that one of their vessels is unloading a cargo,—maybe slaves,—and they don't want us to see it."

"Silence, gentlemen," came La Roux's voice. "Now it's your turn."

Captain Robe's hands were bound tightly behind him and the bandage was passed over his eyes. He knew he was being lifted over the side into one of the waiting boats, perhaps into the river. But his feet struck the boat bottom, and directly the oar dip began, while a low Spanish song arose amid laughter, for the men were well pleased with their capture. Perhaps it was the rhyme of the jolly rover, of the wild life of the high seas. It rose and fell, now in melodious notes, again in a strange, incoherent jingle. And then they were still, save for now and then a muttered word and the oar dip or a bird or brute cry from the thickets. So a half hour must have passed before the boat pushed softly against a muddy beach.

A hand was thrust under Kit's arms, and he arose and stepped, with that guiding hand, over the side on a plank, and then, without a word, he was led some distance, and finally up a step to a room, and, it seemed, in a long passage.

"Sit down," said a voice in English.

As he obeyed, the bandage was removed and he found La Roux's jeering eyes on him, while another untied his hands. The room was large, with small, heavily-barred windows near the ceiling; furnished with a bundle of clean grass as a bed; the stool, where he was sitting; a single low door of heavy iron, slightly ajar, showed a dark corridor.

The fellow who had untied Robe's arms stood as if waiting an order. A pistol was in the sash at his waist, a rough cutlass by his side. His calves and feet were brown and bare. He seemed ready for La Roux's order to end Robe then and there. La Roux himself was dressed in much the same way, save shoes with silver buckles. He regarded the captive with a slight sneer. Robe noted what a handsome young fellow he was, smooth-shaven, with a certain air of breeding, if, as well, of devil-may-care.

"Ah, that remains with you," said Robe with an affected carelessness, remembering that this was his best manner under the cirstances. "You might say to Mr. Lafitte that I await his pleasure."

"Mr. Lafitte will doubtless hear of this," said La Roux with a smile.

"If he didn't order it," Robe began.

"If he didn't order it," the little Baratarian said, quietly. "I have tried to make you and Major Cafferty as comfortable as possible by giving you separate rooms. Your men are in the big room. Our calaboose is not so commodious as I should wish."

"Well, I must wait your or your master's pleasure," Robe said, feeling to know if the documents he bore had not been disturbed.

"I will see that you have some dinner."

"Not now," said Robe, rising. "We ate at Mr. Brownell's, as you doubtless know."

He was thinking of his meeting with Louis Ronald.

"Well, au revoir, my dear captain," said La Roux, turning and motioning the man out.

Suddenly he faced.

"At least you are a brave man, Captain Robe, and, if you'll believe me, you have a friend in Pierre La Roux."

La Roux extended his hand. The sarcastic smile was gone. "No harm will come to you and yours, believe me."

What could have been stranger than to find all this graceful consideration in an officer of the pirates? The captive took the thin, nervous hand,—moulded like a gentleman's, —and their manners were quite as if this were a social occasion. La Roux turned with a slight bow and followed his man. The bolts slipped to their places, and Robe was left to consider the situation. Through the high-barred windows came the mutter of the Louisianian September day.

"It will be only a detention," Robe thought. "They will take me to Lafitte finally. It is probably, as Cafferty surmised, because they are unloading a cargo."

But at that moment there was a low, confused roar, as of many voices, ever nearer, and Robe could distinguish French and Spanish mingled with half-English jargon. What did it mean? Suddenly two shots rang out in rapid succession. The passage seemed filled with shuffling, pushing men, incoherent cries.

Robe braced himself against the wall and bared his arms, determined at least to fight.

The bolts rasped in their sockets. The door was thrown wide on the swearing, jostling crowd, on cutlasses thrust forward, on one tall, sinewy, bare-legged individual who shouted out something in a tongue Robe didn't understand. He must have made a strange picture as he stood there against the brick wall, ready to defend himself. The leader stared at him for a moment and then called back something to the men, whom he had been holding. A half dozen, blear- and red-eyed, rough counterparts of the leader, rushed in at the word and held the cutlass points at the prisoner's breast. Seeing that bare arms had small favor with steel, he folded them and faced his assailants defiantly, while from the corridor the cries continued. The leader motioned the cutlasses down, with a remark that excited laughter. Then, advancing to Robe, he put his hand on his shoulder roughly. Raising his fist, Robe brought the man down. The cutlasses were extended again, but the leader suddenly was on his feet, and, with a leering face, made a motion about his neck, when, with shouts of laughter, the cutlasses were lowered.

"That means I am to be hung," said Robe, calmly. "Well, be good enough to let me walk out to that end."

"You're a cool un," said the leader, with a certain admiration. For a certain deference instead of resentment had followed Robe's blow.

"At least you talk English," said the prisoner.

"I'm an Italian, but I've served on English ships."

"An American or English captain will make you walk the plank yet."

"Maybe," he assented, but showing no greater resentment than such an assault brought out in its leader.

CHAPTER VI

THE WARD OF LAFITTE AND CAPTAIN DOMINIQUE YOU

They came, pushing and jostling, laughing and swearing, from the dark passages into the sunny glare of a glade edged by cypresses.

In the gesticulating throng of drunken men, black, yellow, white, Robe failed to see a single face he remembered as being of his original captors.

The prisoners were arranged in the middle of the circle; the crew of the sloop, his and Cafferty's escort of six men, Simon Wesley's dark, chattering face. Cafferty himself seemed as calm as Robe.

But the men were looking at the half-dozen halters suspended from the trees. They understood that their time had come; that there was but a step to that eternity which awes, yet which never should make a brave man flinch; there are so many better and braver than we on that other side. The fear of death to Kit is the fear of reaching that goal by lingering illness. Yet it was a fearsome thing to die, as they now seemed likely to, in this far-away piratical nest. They might be avenged, but what would that be to them?—small satisfaction when you may be dead. Life and its sweetness suddenly appealed to Robe as never before. He thought of all the pleasures it had given him; yes, he had known a pleasant life; and now—— But he must not let these cattle see that he trembled.

Some of the motley crew were testing the ropes, looking about for the jeering approval of their comrades. The leader, the man whom Robe had felled, strode into the middle of the circle, bowing mockingly to the prisoners, and addressing his comrades with a speech that excited shouts and more laughter. At the end two men advanced towards Cafferty, to whom the leader pointed.

"'Twill be your turn next, Leonardo," Dennis said defiantly to the leader, who turned and translated this, with many comments, to his men. As he was speaking,—while the two men with Dennis were pausing to listen,—a woman, pale, yellow-haired, fair, suddenly burst through the circle, which opened for her; the voice paused; the throng fell suddenly silent as if awed; the two men by Cafferty slunk away from their prisoner.

"De Bertrand!" a voice said, shrilly.

"De Bertrand!" the low shout was repeated. Leonardo himself bent his head. The name De Bertrand was talismanic. And the girl entered there, stood in the circle pale, trembling, her blue eyes flashing; and her voice was in French:

"Back to your ships!" she cried. "Back to your ships, wretches! as you would save your lives."

And Robe stood there in sheer amazement; for the girl, in a simple gown, such as he had seen her wear many times in Virginia, was she whom he had known as his neighbor, his comrade. He had a memory of her at a dance at Georgetown; he heard the full, womanly voice, light with laughter. Was this indeed she?—this slight, rigid, commanding figure before whom these men shrank? And how came she here? And why should they shrink in fear before her, with that word, De Bertrand, explaining all to them, so little to him?

At the moment a short, sturdy, swarthy man ran into the circle. Without a word he drew a pistol from his belt, and with its butt raised advanced to Leonardo, who faced him silently. Neither said a word. But the pistol-butt was raised, and Leonardo fell over like a wooden thing. The new-comer waved his arm, still without a word, and the crowd slunk away as if by magic. Only two turned back and lifted their leader, who lay stunned, perhaps dead. In the confusion the girl in some way disappeared. Robe saw her head in the crowd for a moment, and then it was hidden. His heart beat violently, in his wonder, his surprise, his impulse to rush after her.

The man who had borne out her demand for the mob's dispersal now called back to some companions, who appeared at a dog-trot, headed by La Roux.

"I am sorry, Mr. Robe," that worthy said, rushing up to Robe. "They overpowered the two men in charge of our calaboose."

But he of the effective pistol-butt interrupted La Roux.

"Major Cafferty knows me, Mr. Robe," he said. "I am Dominique You, at your very good service. I will take you at once to Mr. Lafitte, who will be pained to hear of these occurrences. They shouldn't have been stopped at first," he said to La Roux.

"I'm to blame, Captain You," La Roux said.

"Belouche was unloading a cargo," Dominique You himself said after this mild reproof to La Roux.

"Belouche's lieutenant, Leonardo, doubtless thought that you were down here for the customs. He's a lawless fellow and a bit crazed by drink. He thought he would give those who interfere with our trade a lesson."

"And De Bertrand?" asked Robe. "Who is he, Captain You?"

"Twenty years ago you wouldn't have asked that question, Monsieur. He has done more harm to Spanish commerce than any privateer captain of the Gulf."

"And Miss Maurice? How came she here?"

"She,—ah, you knew her in Virginia. She's the ward of Jean Lafitte."

"The ward of Jean Lafitte!" Robe cried; "the ward of her uncle, Philip Maurice!"

"Mr. Lafitte will explain. I can say no more, Mr. Robe," Dominique You went on. "Now, Major Cafferty, your men are quite free. They'll be taken to your sloop and La Roux will see they are entertained."

Robe was rather fearful that Cafferty would display temper, as, indeed, he had good reason. But the revenue officer, who was at the same time a major of the Louisiana militia, met Dominique You's adroit addresses with a calm politeness.

As Kit looks back on his first meeting with this remarkable man, Dominique You, he remembers that captain's subsequent career, so strange in contrast with its begin-

CHALMETTE

ning. He remembers the monument to him in New Orleans, and that the city never gave another of its citizens so great a funeral display. And so he feels called on to record his own surprise at this remarkable mixture of a man of action and of address. Dominique You never had the subtlety of either of the Lafittes. But the three were by far the most extraordinary men among Kit's acquaintances, barring, perhaps, General Jackson.

They came out of the woodland into the most charming rural scene; handsome and well-kept villas, as fine as any about New Orleans; people coming and going about quiet vocations; the bay, with its many smaller sails and three large vessels at anchor; the landing places active; great warehouses lining the shore. As they passed on, men exchanged salutations with Captain You. Their path led back of this scene of activity, among orange groves, past well-kept farms, and about all was the marvel of light and color,—of the sea and land and the cloud-flecked sky. Cafferty pointed out a line of barges which he said plied constantly between the La Fourche and the Mississippi, and Robe began to understand how great was the trade of Barataria; how here was centred much of the commerce of the Mississippi Valley.

They came at last to a house, where Dominique You exchanged some words with a black servant, and directly were ushered through a hall, as fine in its appointments as any Robe had seen, into a small room where a man sat dictating to a secretary.

As they entered he arose. Robe saw again Jean Lafitte.

"This is a pleasure, Captain Robe," said he. "How is our friend, Mr. Deschamps,— and Major Cafferty, too?"

"I have been apologizing for some indignities these gentlemen have suffered," Dominique You said.

"Ah, that too zealous La Roux!" Lafitte said.

"No, worse; Belouche's crew came near hanging 'em," Captain You continued.

"Oh, this is atrocious," Mr. Lafitte said,

with a fine show of surprise. "How may we apologize enough? You know we are made up of so many wild characters,—it's sometimes unavoidable."

Mr. Robe assured him that he quite understood, and he went on to say that he bore some letters from General Jackson himself, while Major Cafferty had like documents from Governor Claiborne.

"I will read them now if you will excuse me," Lafitte said.

He handed the papers over to his secretary, who read the documents in a low tone. Dominique You, as if these had no particular interest to him, rose with a nod and went out.

At last Lafitte said,—

"As usual, we are summoned to disperse by all authorities. Well, I don't think,— we will."

His voice came out low, positive, while he smiled urbanely on his two visitors. He paused for a moment.

"It would not be for the interest of Louisiana to have us scattered. Your General Jackson will need us later. I can put five hundred armed men in the field, gentlemen,—men who understand guns, who are not afraid of death,—desperate, tried men."

For another moment he paused, and then began again with a gentle, persuasive voice :

"Say what you will, to what does New Orleans owe prosperity so much as to the trade of Barataria? Call us names, but do not forget that we, the leaders, are patriots. Tell that to your General Jackson. Yet wait, there may be something more to say. I will consult with the captains. In the mean time I will try to make up to you for your detention,—in some poor way."

And again he paused, looking the two visitors over shrewdly, as if noting the effect of his words.

"The courts have decided in our favor. Yet we must be persecuted. Ah, Major Cafferty, I suspect that there are many in New Orleans who would like to be part of an expedition against Barataria. They think we have some riches here."

"That is undoubtedly true," Dennis answered.

As he spoke a report rang out, such as may be from a ship's gun.

Lafitte turned to his secretary, who looked a young Spanish student. As he went out hurriedly, the master turned.

"I must follow him. That gun signifies something."

"Yes," said Cafferty, when Lafitte had gone. "There's a ship outside,—a warship."

"It might be one of those privateers."

"Yes, we can't tell. But I believe it was unexpected."

"What did Dominique You mean by describing Miss Maurice as the ward of Lafitte? How does she happen to be here? Why did those fellows stop when she spoke?" Robe asked.

Again the gun rang out.

"The second summons," Cafferty said, eagerly. "As for the girl,—you know her?"

"She is from the estate adjoining Westmore."

"It's strange," Dennis said. "Let me think. They said 'De Bertrand.' She is identified with the old pirate in some way."

"With De Bertrand?" Robe asked. "How can she be?"

The door was pushed open. A black stood outside.

"I come for the gentleman who represents General Jackson," he said.

"I am he," Robe said.

"Come with me, sir," the man said.

"And I am to leave you, Dennis."

"I don't see that we can be choosers,— at present," Dennis said. And Robe followed the man.

Outside he noticed a gayly-fitted barge putting out from one of the wharves, and he thought there seemed some excitement in a crowd gathered there since his companion and he had entered the house. A figure in the barge looked Lafitte's.

"Is that Mr. Lafitte's barge?"

"Oui, M'sieur," said the negro.

He led to a house possibly one-eighth of

a mile farther. There the door swung back as if they were expected. The guide knocked gently at a door, which opened, and Robe was aware of a great room,—dim, for the curtains were closely drawn; of a bed, where a strange, gaunt figure was propped with pillows.

CHAPTER VII

THE DEATH-BED OF DE BERTRAND

The man was very old; his face thin, bony, yet commanding; the eyes sunken, yet searching and bright,—with the brightness approaching death sometimes gives old person's eyes. Now he motioned to a chair, while his voice came out thin, rasping:

"Ye are from the general and the governor?"

"Yes, sir," said Robe, involuntarily giving age a tribute.

"Tell them, then, that ye saw Felix de Bertrand — they called me, the English, the Pirate—on his dying bed Tell them they must not disregard what I say. And I say, for the good of Louisiana, take Jean Lafitte at his word."

"I will so report," Robe said, bowing his head, for age and death sat together with him in that room.

"And tell them that I repent nothing. My life has been war,—war for myself. But when I held the Gulf, at least, my authority was respected. Now Jean Lafitte, a greater man, has taken my place. And I die, not fearing, but ready before God to say, 'I have done what I have done.'"

And Robe bowed his head, realizing how bloody that life had been, how tainted with crime, and yet respecting the bravery acknowledging it all. The voice had become strong and clear, and now added:

"That is all, my friend."

"I will deliver it word for word, as you have said it," Robe said.

"Eh," said the voice querulously, " word for word. I like your face, my friend. Give me your hand, if you'll take De Bertrand's hand."

As Robe took the cold, bony hand he felt nearer to death than he himself ever had been. And then he heard from the shadow of the bed a low sobbing, and he distinguished a woman's kneeling figure. "Was it she?" he asked.

"Be quiet, lass," said the old man, "you're the last,—you and Madeleine."

"Yes, grandfather."

And the voice was Sallie Maurice's, the tone that had been his playmate's.

"Show him out, lass," said De Bertrand. "Let him know that we in Barataria are not without hospitality."

And the eyes closed, and Robe went to the door, past the three slaves, the man and two women, who stood with bowed heads.

As he hesitated in the hall, "He told me to follow you," she said

"And would you not of your own will."

"No, Christopher Robe."

"But there has been that between us,— though not all spoken,—which should have made you, Sallie Maurice."

"That is so; Kit, we were playfellows, and you had a right."

"What right? Oh, the note you sent me. I understand now; I was foolish. But that is over, please. It was but a fancy."

"Don't touch me. The man I care for shall have no fancies. But"—her voice grew calm—"he is my mother's father. Sister Madeleine of the Ursulines was my mother's sister. They sent for me when they knew he couldn't be better. My uncle was opposed to it, but I would come."

"I like you for it."

"Could I have done else? My father met my mother, his daughter, in Martinique. And when she died my father brought me to Virginia, where he died of the fever,—that is the story, Kit."

And Kit remembered what his father had said of the bad blood of the Maurices. Why had he never known of that story? He was to learn later that no one knew of Reginald Maurice's wife as De Bertrand's daughter.

"You saved my life. You must have cared, the way you rushed out among those rough men," he said.

"It was Captain You. And then I didn't know you were there. I simply heard that Belouche and his men had started to hang some revenue officers, and I ran down there."

"Ah, it was daring of you," he said.

"They know me as a De Bertrand."

"Dear——" he began.

"You must not," she said.

"I must not wish to take you,—in my arms,—to tell you——"

"No, no," she said. "I won't hear you talk in that way. And even if I wanted to allow it, I wouldn't,—the pirate's granddaughter and a Robe of Westmore!" and she laughed softly.

"You have half-confessed," Kit insisted. "I love you, dear. I love you."

"And that other girl——?"

"That girl!" he said. "Who told you?"

"Ah, there was something to tell," she cried. "Well, I have very good authority,—no less than Mr. Ronald's."

"That fellow,—you know him?"

"I think him very nice."

"Eh, you do? He will hear from me. Are you safe here,—in this place?"

"They are my grandfather's people," she said, with a certain ring of pride.

"And you are Jean Lafitte's ward?"

"He manages my grandfather's property," she said. For a moment they were silent.

"I wish I could do something," he said.

"What did I tell you to do when you left Virginia?"

"My part."

"Do it now,—in this trouble,—this war which will visit us here."

"Will it please you?"

"Yes, as much as anything may."

A door opened and no less a person than La Roux entered. He glanced from Miss Maurice to Robe.

"Mr. Lafitte sends for you, sir."

"You must go," she said.

"I shall see you again before I leave Barataria."

"You must not expect that," she said. "They will not let you."

"Why?"

"I don't wish it."

"You?" he asked.

"Yes, I."

"I shall make you wish it," Robe said. "That is all. There will be another day for us, Sallie."

And he followed La Roux.

CHAPTER VIII

THE ENTERTAINMENT TO HIS MAJESTY'S OFFICERS

"Mr. Lafitte bids you to his board. He has prepared a slight entertainment for some British officers."

"British officers?" Robe said. "The guns we heard were from a British vessel——?"

"From the brig Norfolk."

What other purpose than one to tempt Lafitte had brought the Norfolk to Barataria? And he began seriously to consider whether, indeed, if the Lafittes were earnest in their protestations of their allegiance to the United States, it might not be better to accept their propositions. But the delicate question was whether they were in earnest. Yet the words and face of the dying man,—for he was sure De Bertrand was dying,—carried to Robe's heart a feeling that Lafitte had been so.

He was taken into a room where he was

told to make ready for the banquet which was prepared. He was surprised at this haste, but he afterwards learned that the arrangements had been made to impress Cafferty and himself, and that the appearance of the British brig was indeed a surprise to Barataria.

While he expected almost any lavish and barbaric display, the dining-room to which he was taken was surprising. The room might have been in any polite centre. The silver was of the rarest designs, and he was to find the most palatable French and Spanish wines, and game and meats of the varieties afforded by the locality.

Cafferty was there with a rather puzzled expression, and the three British officers, a grizzled captain who had served with Nelson, Lieutenant the Earl of Burnham, and a fair young lieutenant whose name Robe lost, though he was placed next him at table.

Lafitte greeted him with the manner of a man of fashion, and certainly his tailor,—for he had dressed for the occasion,—was excellent.

"You have been to my old friend, De Bertrand," he said. "He can't live."

"I was much surprised with him," Robe said. "I find his granddaughter and I are old acquaintances."

"Oh, Miss Maurice," Lafitte said, and he looked at Robe keenly. "I had forgotten that my introduction to you came through Philip Maurice. Now, will you sit down, gentlemen?"

From that moment he charmed his guests, who looked on him with wonder. And, in fact, it needs not Kit's testimony to declare the grace, the wordliness of this man, who, whatever his past, had the most delightful manners of any gentleman of Kit's acquaintance.

"We might be in England," said the young gentleman at Robe's side. "I am not so much surprised, since I have been in New Orleans."

"Have you?" said Robe, absently.

"Yes, before the war. We were chasing pirates. We tried to chase you fellows since, but, I say, you have put up some splendid fights. We appreciate your sailors."

"Yes," said Robe, quietly; "I, too, am proud of them, and when the tribute comes from you it's all the more forcible."

"Oh, you forced us to it with your Lawrences and your Perrys. Nor am I proud of the burning of Washington. I fancy we'll be at you down here directly."

"Yes," said Robe, "we expect that."

"You are well divided up,—Spaniards for Spain, French for France, and pirates——"

He looked about significantly.

"I have changed my mind about 'em. Money gives even pirates a manner, though that man has breeding. I declare, you wouldn't suspect him of the bloody truth. Now isn't it cunning of him? We are both down here on a mission, I fancy. He lets us see that he is negotiating on both sides and puts up his price. He dines us both together."

"I wonder if that is the case?" said Robe. "By the way, you know I lost your name."

"I am doing it always myself,—Beaumont."

"And you were in New Orleans before the war? You know Deschamps and the De Reniers?"

"You know Mademoiselle Marie!" the young officer cried.

"I indeed do, and we have talked of you."

"She remembers me, eh?"

"I think you made a decided impression."

"Don't flatter me. She's a nice little girl. But isn't this odd,—that we should meet? How is she?"

"As pretty as ever," said Robe. "I think she always must have been, you know."

"Well, she was, and when we take your New Orleans I will pay her a visit."

"Oh, perhaps we will take you up there," said Captain Robe.

"Oh, well, you have a lot of picked up troops against veterans."

"Yes, I allow that," said Robe. "It's a grave question."

But then a sally of the host interrupted

CHALMETTE

this low talk. Robe had taken a great liking to Beaumont. He wondered if he had better tell him of his own sentimental escapade with Mademoiselle. Oh, that unfortunate escapade! And he thought of the girl in the nearby house with the dying chief.

And that remarkable dinner went on. As Kit recalls it now, he wonders if it is quite believable, though it was his own experience. Yet he finds it written of in the histories, and there are many living to corroborate the story.

Finally, the cigars were brought. (It must be remarked that the service was excellent, the black servants well trained.)

"I am going to ask Captain Robe and Major Cafferty to leave us here over the cigars," Lafitte said. "It seems there's a little private matter to talk about."

The British captain looked suspiciously at the Americans as they rose.

"He's wondering what it all means," said Dennis; "I am wondering myself. Let's walk down along the wharves, if they don't stop us."

"They are not here to warn them that they will be driven out of Barataria."

"They are here to bribe them for the British service," Cafferty assented.

"Yes," said Robe. "Dennis, tell me of De Bertrand."

"The old pirate?"

"Yes."

"Well, I thought everybody knew. The story runs that seventy-five years ago a French merchantman was scuttled, and of all the crew a boy, known as De Bertrand, was saved. 'Tis a romantic story enough. There was no trace of his parentage. He grew up on the seas. He became the Pirate Bertrand, who was the worst of them all. He made an organization of them before Lafitte's time. And in some way he was always carrying some government's flag as a privateer; he was always escaping positive proof. And now he's old, and, they say, fabulously rich. It's a disgrace to Louisiana that they should be nested here," Dennis ended, in a burst of anger.

"He had two daughters. I don't know

what became of one, but they say the other is a nun of the Ursulines. What did they want of you?"

"De Bertrand wanted to see me," Robe said.

"You saw him, the old pirate?"

"He is dying."

"Dying, eh? He has made many men die."

"Yes, he's a dying man. He sent to tell me that General Jackson had better accept Lafitte's offer."

"That must have been impressive—from a dying man," Cafferty remarked. It had impressed Robe, as you know, but he did not mention having seen Miss Maurice there.

At this moment La Roux came toward them.

"I am instructed to ask you in here," he said, pointing to a low house, "to await Mr. Lafitte."

As they followed, Cafferty muttered, "What do you think will be next?"

La Roux left them in a room by a window, where they had a view of the bay and the shipping. He did not say a word further, nor did the two attempt to question him as with a nod he left them, closing the door.

CHAPTER IX

THE DIPLOMACY OF LAFITTE

As they watched at the window, gravely discussing the situation, they saw on a path the three British officers. Suddenly from behind one of the warehouses there rushed out a score of those gesticulating, red-and-white turbaned, bare-legged fellows, such as had seized them; and the three officers of his Majesty's brig were last seen,—fighting, and then accepting the inevitable.

"It's our story over," said Robe. "They have enjoyed Lafitte's hospitality, and now they have a chance to consider another side of the question,—'pirates or gentlemen?'—hem!"

"I picked out our friend La Roux in the crowd," Cafferty said; "the same fellow, exactly. My eyes are good."

"I wonder, Dennis, why——?"

But a slow, modulated voice interrupted, and turning they saw Jean Lafitte, whom they had not noticed enter.

"His Majesty's officers are receiving the same attention as we," said Robe.

Lafitte did not attempt to deny his knowledge of the occurrence, though he lifted his hands in pretended astonishment.

"Ah, these unruly fellows," he said. "They are continually trying my patience. Now I shall have to explain to the captain of the Norfolk as I did to you. But they can wait for the present. I have now something to say to you."

He paused, and then went on almost exactly with the same phrasing that he afterwards used in a certain well-known letter to Governor Claiborne :—

"Though proscribed in my adopted country, I will never miss an opportunity of serving her, or of proving that she has never ceased to be dear to me. I may have evaded the payment of duties to the custom-house, but I never have ceased to be a good citizen, and all my offences, such as they are, have been forced on me by certain vices of the law."

Cafferty smiled ironically, knowing this phrase-maker better than Robe, who was, indeed, considerably impressed.

"Now I will show you what this leads to," and he handed Robe a packet of despatches. "You will find a letter from the British commander at Pensacola."

"I may show them to Cafferty?" Robe asked.

"Of course," said Lafitte, taking a chair and crossing his legs, and awaiting the effect of the papers on his guests with apparent indifference.

Robe read Cafferty an offer to pay to Jean Lafitte thirty thousand dollars, either in Pensacola or New Orleans; to give him an army captaincy; to secure the enlistment of his men in the British navy. A printed pamphlet accompanied this calling on the Louisianians "to rise and liberate their paternal soil from a faithless and imbecile government."

"You are considering these overtures?" the revenue officer said, at last.

"Well, I am not a man to neglect diplomacy. I have told Captain Brown that I must lay the matter before certain of my captains."

"And you have arrested the British officers?" Cafferty said.

But Lafitte interrupted with a fine show of scorn:

"They are my guests, as you are. They shall be freed in a moment. I will escort them to their brig. But, as for these papers, you can see that your enemy considers the Baratarians of some importance."

"And you?" Robe asked, slowly.

"Many of our friends advise the British allegiance. How can you hold this State with the means at your disposal?"

"But you, sir?"

The man looked at them intently, and then his voice came out again, slow and measured:

"You may assure the governor and the general that I offer to restore to the State certain citizens, who will be ready to do their utmost for the common defence. The only reward I ask is that a stop be put on the persecution against me and my supporters. Yet, whether my offer be refused or accepted, I will refuse the British."

The two listeners said nothing, when Lafitte added, rather coldly,—

"That is all. I can say no more. Your sloop is ready now."

"We shall carefully report your words, Mr. Lafitte," Cafferty said.

"And I for my part will state my belief that your proposition should be accepted," Robe put in. "You say our men are ready. Well, allow me to say that I for one have appreciated your hospitality."

Lafitte inclined his head.

"La Roux," he called, when the door opened, showing that individual, whom Cafferty thought he had seen in the attack on the British officers. La Roux smiled mockingly at them.

"You will escort Captain Robe and Major Cafferty to their sloop, and see that their men are satisfied with their treatment."

"I wish, if I may," said Robe, hesitatingly, "to pay my respects to Miss Maurice."

"Ah, yes, you know Captain de Bertrand's granddaughter," said Lafitte, quickly. "I first met you through an introduction from Philip Maurice," he added, repeating what he had said at the dinner.

"Yes, Mr. Lafitte. I suppose——" and he hesitated. He was going to say that he supposed it was safe for Miss Maurice in Barataria. But he did not commit that indiscretion.

"La Roux," said Lafitte, slowly, "take Mr. Robe to Captain de Bertrand's. But do not wait there too long. I wish these two to be on the river again before the officers of the Norfolk are released. I shall have to apologize to them."

"And I am obliged, sir," said Captain Robe, again. "I have told you what my report shall be."

"And mine, sir," said Cafferty, as they followed La Roux outside.

"You didn't tell me of this Miss Maurice?" he added to his companion.

"I really didn't," Robe replied. "She is De Bertrand's granddaughter."

"And so is part of the Lafitte establishment. She probably will inherit a considerable property from De Bertrand. Lafitte looked at you with some dislike when you asked the question."

"You think that?"

"I know, and he rarely betrays a thought by look or action. I have been thinking how shrewd he is. He will end, through this war, in getting restored to citizenship."

They were talking in low tones, La Roux a little ahead of them. At last he stopped before the De Bertrand house.

"I can let you have ten minutes, sir," La Roux said. "Major Cafferty and I will wait you outside."

The black servant at the door hesitated when he asked for Miss Maurice, but finally he consented to inquire. He had the strictest orders, he added, that she should see no one at all, save Mr. Lafitte and Mr. Ronald, who was expected from New Orleans. Robe started at this last name. This man had told her of his affair with Mademoiselle de Renier, and he was expected here.

"And more, sir, Captain de Bertrand died a half-hour since."

Lafitte had not known that when he permitted the visit. The old man must have died shortly after Robe had left her.

"Please to give Miss Maurice my sympathy," he said, in a changed voice. "If she can see me, I should like it. I am Christopher Robe; your mistress will know."

In a few moments the man returned and bade him in. He was conscious that the ten minutes La Roux had allowed him must be near passed.

She was awaiting him in a room at the right of the hall. Her voice was grave and listless and her eyes sad.

"I am glad you came again," she said, softly.

"I wish I might take you away."

"No, no; but you can do me a favor in New Orleans. You can go to the Ursulines and see my aunt. I am glad I came here. My instinct about it was right."

"Yes, I am sure it was," Robe agreed. But—I hate to leave you here."

"I am as safe here as anywhere in the world. I am in Mr. Lafitte's charge."

Robe felt jealous of Lafitte; he was so handsome, so charming; and there was this Ronald.

"Ronald is interested in the Baratarians," he said.

"Yes," she acknowledged.

"Pardon me," came the black's voice; "Monsieur La Roux says he must hurry you."

He took her hand.

"I shall see you in New Orleans?" he said.

"I don't know even that."

"But I shall keep on telling you what I have."

"Hush!" she said. "There is that other girl, Kit?" she added, with a little laugh.

"Bother that other girl!" he said. "I have a great mind to kiss you,—to make you take back your words."

"And then to think of it," she said, "the pirate's granddaughter——"

"You foolish girl, you said that once before. What do I care for that, or anything? It's you,—you alone."

"You must go now. You have your duty. They will not let you stay here longer."

"I will tell them what he told me," Robe said. "I mustn't bother you more now."

Again he took her hand, which she did not withdraw, and then, leaving her, he went out to La Roux and Cafferty.

"The captain is dead," said La Roux, awed.

"The captain is dead," said Robe.

What would this mean to Sallie Maurice? what to him, now that she was identified with these lawless men? Yet he certainly couldn't take her away now. And then he remembered Sister Madeleine, to whom he bore the message. She, perhaps, could tell him more; and he would tell her frankly his own position.

CHAPTER X

MONSIEUR CLEMENT

THE wind, as well as the current, was against them, and the sloop made slow progress. The men were in the best of humors, and had forgotten, in their subsequent reception, the indignities and dangers of the earlier one. Robe was silent. The events of the Baratarian visit seemed like a dream,—the strange complications surrounding one whom he had always known. And yet he felt it was all real enough; and he wondered in apprehension of what the sequel would prove.

They stopped the first night at Mr. Brownell's, who was much interested in the result of their mission, though they were not at liberty to tell him. Robe asked him if he thought that his neighbor, Ronald, had not sent on the word which led to their reception at Barataria. Mr. Brownell said this was probable; Ronald, like so many others, was hand-in-glove with the Baratarians.

"His mother was an Englishwoman, and he has lived much in England," said Robe, remembering that story. And he wondered how far Ronald's influence would be exerted to have the Lafittes accept the English proposal.

"Ronald's wealth, his fame as a duellist,—he has killed three men,—make him a man to be cultivated by the Lafittes," Brownell said. "Who is there in Louisiana who is not in their interest? I sometimes ask. They own the Legislature, body and soul, and Cafferty knows you can't get the militia to fight them. Do ye remember the argument once advanced, that it would be fighting France; that Jean Lafitte had letters-of-marque from Napoleon?"

"I shall see the day when the place is burned down," said Cafferty, moodily.

"The governor has sent out the old proclamation," said Mr. Brownell; "five hundred dollars for Jean or Pierre Lafitte's arrest,—a thousand for both. They can't put their hands on Pierre this time."

"But they have been cleared by the courts!" Robe cried.

"It's another act," said Brownell. "The news is down here; a revenue collector, Doane, was shot last week by Lafitte's order."

"We came near being hung," said Robe; and he told the story of their own experience with Belouche's crew. Cafferty added the episode of the interruption by De Bertrand's granddaughter and Captain Dominique You when Robe was silent. This news of the death of the collector seemed to stir up Cafferty considerably, and he swore a little.

"You mustn't forget the situation and the messages we have to deliver," said Robe.

But the next afternoon they had a strange adventure, which indicated that Jean Lafitte perhaps did not trust them entirely for a dispassionate representation of his position.

Cafferty had been asked by Governor Claiborne to stop at the plantation of a Madame Demarche, and to offer to escort Mrs. Claiborne, who was stopping there, to the city. They reached Madame Demarche's about three of the afternoon of the day after leaving Mr. Brownell's,—the wind having continued persistently against them. They expected to reach the city about nine that night.

Robe accompanied Cafferty to the house-door. Dennis remarked that the place seemed deserted. A trim mulatto girl came to the door, it seemed nervously.

"My respects to Madame, Henriette," Cafferty said. "Is Madame Claiborne here?"

"Oui, M'sieur."

"Will you announce me and Captain Robe. The governor suggested that I stop here on my way to the city."

"I will see, M'sieur; they are dining."

"Don't let us interrupt."

"I'll see, M'sieur," said the girl again. "Come in, Messieurs," she said, returning.

It was Madame Demarche who greeted them, also rather embarrassed, Cafferty afterwards said from his knowledge of this charming lady.

Oh, Madame was going to keep Madame Claiborne another day,—another day.

"Monsieur Clement wishes to see Madame for a moment," said Henriette, at the door.

Madame begged to be excused and ran out, and returned directly, pale, anxious-eyed.

"He says I need not fear you. But you are officers?"

"What may it be, Madame?" Dennis asked.

"Oh, Monsieur, this Monsieur Clement is Monsieur Jean Lafitte."

"Jean Lafitte!" Cafferty cried. "We left him at Barataria."

And Robe, whose ear was more wonted to French, understood. Jean Lafitte here as soon as they? And then he remembered that Lafitte might have come by a shorter way, for who knew the devious windings of the bayous better than he? But Madame, having confessed, went on:

"You won't hurt him, Monsieur Cafferty; he says you won't,—that you have a message from him to the governor. He has a price on his head. And he came here at noon to-day. He said he was on his way to the city. I said, 'Monsieur, you must not go there. You must return at once. Your life, I tell you, is in danger.' You know Monsieur Lafitte, he laughed at me, and who should enter just then but my guest, Mrs. Claiborne? What could I do? I introduced him as Monsieur Clement, and then I went out of the room and called Henriette. 'Henriette,' said I, 'Governor Claiborne has put a price on M. Lafitte's head. Any one who delivers him to the government will receive five hundred dollars, and Monsieur's head will be cut off. Send the servants and the children away. Set the table and wait yourselves, and remember Monsieur is Monsieur Clement.' Now you come, and he directs me to tell you he is here."

"He need not fear us till after our report to the governor," said Dennis.

"I can believe you, Monsieur?"

"You can believe me, Madame," Dennis replied.

Madame then asked them in. Mr. Lafitte

recognized them with a nod, and they addressed him as M. Clement. Mrs. Claiborne, who never looked more beautiful,—she was one of the handsomest women Robe ever knew,—seemed much interested in M. Clement, whose talk fairly sped. His wit never was more entertaining, his manner never more delightful, and he seemed to them all a splendid gentleman.

"You are to escort me back to the city," Mrs. Claiborne said. "Ah, Captain Robe, I have been singing your praises,—what is my reward?—to a young lady you are interested in."

"Who may that be, Madame?" said M. Clement, urbanely.

"Mademoiselle Marie de Renier," said Madame Claiborne, smiling at Robe, who found himself flushing. He wanted to get a word to Lafitte, and he succeeded while they were waiting for Madame to make ready.

"I saw Miss Maurice," he said, "thanks to you. And I regretted to learn of Captain de Bertrand's death."

"Miss Maurice is now in my care," Lafitte

returned, curtly, "unless she returns to Mr. Maurice in Virginia. Eh, sir, you seem to have several interests in the sex."

"Mademoiselle de Renier?" Robe said. "Oh, that was but women's talk."

"I saw our friends on board their brig, after due apology," Lafitte went on. "Now I am on my way——"

"To the city? It's dangerous for you there."

"Oh, not after your report," he answered. "Ah, here is Madame. I envy the governor."

The governor's lady and M. Clement seemed to have an interesting parting, and she was loud in her praises of the gentleman she had met, plying the two with questions about him. Why hadn't she known him before? Wasn't he entertaining? To all of which Robe and Cafferty agreed, without letting her know that M. Clement was that dangerous outlaw, Jean Lafitte. So they came to the city, Robe very quiet and Mrs. Claiborne doubtless voting him stupid.

The two accompanied her to the governor's house. Late as it was, Governor Claiborne was awake and busy.

"Well?" he said, turning.

Cafferty went over their experiences and Robe corroborated them.

"The British!" the governor cried. "I thought as much. And you saw him,—with the price on him,—so near as Madame Demarche's,—and my wife met him?"

"She thinks him a Monsieur Clement."

"I shall not undeceive her. I'll try to get at her impression. Now what do you advise, Captain Robe?"

"I would accept his offer," Robe said.

"And you, major?"

"I wouldn't," said Cafferty. "Make no terms with such law violators."

"We in Louisiana are not in a strong position," said the governor, quietly. "But I'll think about it. Be here at nine in the morning, Captain Robe, and I will give you my conclusions to carry to General Jackson."

Robe left Cafferty without many words; he was inclined to quarrel with that worthy's conclusion. Simon Wesley was awaiting him sleepily after the episodes of that exciting journey. As for the master, though perplexed and troubled about several matters, he fell into dreamless sleep, to be awakened by Simon Wesley about nine in the morning. He dressed, ate a light breakfast, and hurried to the governor's.

In the corridor he met Mrs. Claiborne, who, looking very lovely indeed at this early hour, was talking with a gentleman. Startled, Robe saw that this was no other than Lafitte.

"Ah, Monsieur, I am charmed to see you," Madame was saying. "You have been announced to my husband?"

"With your permission, I am on my way there."

Robe hesitated. Had Lafitte been bidden to New Orleans by the governor? Or had the subtle man decided to bring his personality to bear on the governor? Robe thought of all this as he hesitated there. Madame's voice reached in on his brief revery.

"My husband expects you as well as

Monsieur Clement," she said, and Robe followed Lafitte. The man had ventured into the lion's den; he might be seized at any moment.

The door opened. Lafitte paused on the threshold while his eyes sought the governor's. Robe paused, Madame, looking curiously in, just behind him.

"Sir," said the man in the doorway, "I am Lafitte."

Never did a man look up with greater astonishment than did Governor Claiborne. Madame gave a scream, and her hand involuntarily clutched Robe's arm.

"Sir?" said the governor, as if not quite understanding.

"One moment, sir," said Lafitte. "You have put a price on my head?"

"On a pirate's head," said Claiborne, studying his visitor's face.

Lafitte advanced into the room. Suddenly from his coat he drew two pistols, cocked and primed.

"I shall do you no harm, Governor Claiborne; I will not so embarrass Madame.

You needn't call on Captain Robe. But I am armed, because if you attempt to detain me, I must try to get to the street.

"Wait, sir," he added; "I have come here voluntarily to make a personal offer of my services to this State against the British. My men are disciplined, brave,—there are none better in any army. Does the State accept? or no?"

The room fell still. Madame, her hand still unconsciously on Robe's arm, looked from Monsieur Clement—this pirate Lafitte!—to her husband, who seemed to be considering the situation,—to be studying this visitor.

"I have Major Cafferty's and Captain Robe's report," he said at last.

"I have nothing to add to that," said Lafitte, slowly, fingering his pistols.

A moment more passed.

"Sir," said the governor at last, "I accept."

"The men, sir, will be at daylight the day after to-morrow awaiting your orders at Madame Demarche's."

Lafitte bowed as he finished, and then

inclined his head to Madame and walked out.

"I think," said the governor, "that now, Captain Robe, you can make your report to General Jackson. You will start this morning."

"Pardon me," said Madame, slowly, her black eyes turning from her husband to Robe; "you knew, Mr. Robe, that he was Lafitte?"

"I knew."

"And Madame Demarche deceived me,— because——"

"Because he had a price on his head," the governor himself explained.

"He hasn't it now?" Madame asked. "He is so handsome!"

"Eh, dear, that pardons a man, or condemns a woman,—with a woman. I knew last night that this Monsieur Clement of yours was Monsieur Lafitte."

"And you never told me?"

"I wanted to see what you thought of him as Clement," said the governor.

"Yet you left me deceived?" said Madame,

with a pout,—"you left me deceived. What if he had never appeared here!"

"Do you think less of him as Lafitte or Clement?" the governor asked.

"If," said Madame, reflectingly, "this meeting hadn't taken place, and you had told me he was Lafitte, I should have held him interesting, even as Lafitte. And now having known him as Clement, again as Lafitte,—for haven't you accepted his offer? —I am inclined to think him a very wonderful and agreeable man."

"I must side with you, my dear," said the governor, "though no man in Louisiana has made me more trouble."

"But wasn't it a delightful adventure!" said Madame, turning to Captain Robe.

CHAPTER XI

THE URSULINE SISTER

Mr. Raoul Deschamps and M. de St. Gëme some two hours after this were returning from their review of the creole company, which M. de St. Gëme commanded, when Deschamps saw his friend, Captain Robe.

"Where have you been?" Deschamps asked. "Ah, I have missed you. And a certain young lady I know has asked after you. M. de St. Gëme, M. Robe," Deschamps continued, speaking French, recognizing Robe's new skill with that tongue. Captain Robe was to know much of this same M. de St. Gëme.

"I have met a friend of hers in Barataria," Robe said. "And you can do me the favor of letting her know that, as I leave the city within an hour for Mobile."

"Who may that be?"

"You remember a Lieutenant Beaumont you told me about?"

"You found a British ship in Barataria!"

"I am told to make it no secret," Robe replied. "The British were approaching Lafitte, and—I have the authority of the governor to make the statement, with the assurance that he fully believes it—Jean Lafitte rejected their propositions."

M. de St. Gëme said he knew that such would be the case. He had every confidence in Jean Lafitte's patriotism; besides, New Orleans needed the assistance of all her fighting men.

"But haven't you time to tell Mademoiselle de Renier in person," Deschamps interrupted, "that her lieutenant was of that ship's company? But I make a shrewd guess myself that our little friend has forgotten everything else in thought of Captain Robe."

"You are mistaken," Robe said, quickly. "Mademoiselle Marie and I understand each other. Do tell her this for me, with my regards. Now one more favor,—can you find out if I can see Jean Lafitte? I believe he must be in New Orleans."

"With the price on his head," Deschamps said; "still, that fact once didn't bother him so much. You wish to see him? I will be at your lodging within the hour."

Robe thanked him for the trouble and then went to pay the visit on the Ursulines he had promised Miss Maurice. He wanted to see Lafitte again before he left New Orleans; he did not know when he might return. He wished to talk with Lafitte about De Bertrand's granddaughter, and yet he hardly knew what he could say. Nor was it quite clear to him what he would talk of at the Ursulines beyond the bare news he had to report of Sister Madeleine's father's death. To carry such news is not at the best pleasing, and he thought how he would better word it as he looked in through the grating at the porter. But when, some moments after, he was in Sister Madeleine's presence, he said simply,—

"I am from Barataria. Captain de Bertrand died three days ago."

"You have been there, sir," she said, and then, more slowly, "he is dead,—my father."

And suddenly she knelt down and prayed, and Robe turned away. When he looked up she sat there, calm and still.

"My niece was there. You know she is my niece?"

"Is it safe for her? Yes, for I bring you her message."

Then quickly, impulsively, he told his own story, not hiding his faults nor the flirtation with Mademoiselle de Renier. Sister Madeleine's face seemed to draw the words from him, whether he would or no,—seemed to lead him on to this confidence. At last she said,—

"I think you straightforward, honest. I told you that before. But we of the De Bertrands have a heavy burden,—a curse."

"He did not fear it,—your father, Felix de Bertrand," he said.

"No, he was no more afraid of death than he was of men," she said proudly. "I wish I had been with my niece. I did not think his case serious, though he was anxious to have her there. In Virginia you were boy and girl together."

"And I don't like to have her misunderstand me about my attentions to some one else," he said.

"Oh, Mademoiselle de Renier," the nun said with a smile; "she was educated with us."

"Girls are so stubborn about some fancies they get into their heads," said Kit.

"You think you understand them?" said the nun, still smiling. "I will tell her that I like you; I am rarely wrong. But as for herself, I don't know positively. She has talked to me about taking the veil."

"Don't let her do that, whatever she may do," Kit said.

"That is between God and her," said the nun, slowly. "I was ashamed in the world, —my father's career made me so,—and I found rest here, and in doing God's work, such as I may. But as for her,—I have seen little of her, Mr. Robe. She was always in Virginia since the time she was taken from Martinique. She was brought up in ignorance of us. She has, I fancy, some of his spirit,—the De Bertrand spirit."

Kit told her of how at Barataria she had ventured to interrupt the crew who intended hanging him and his companions. The nun listened, her chin on her hand.

"Yes, his spirit."

"But is she safe there? What will Lafitte do? Is he to be trusted?"

"She has a great fortune,—gained, you know how. I would have none of it from my father. Monsieur Lafitte might wish to arrange her marriage to further best his own plans; he has done such things. As for her, I don't believe she even knows about the money."

"And Lafitte?"

"You are jealous of him?"

"I hardly know."

"You are not sure of her?" said the nun, slowly. "No, how can you be? Yet she rushed among those rough men when she heard you were to be hurt."

"She would have done that, naturally, for any one."

"Yes, perhaps," Sister Madeleine said, as if doubtfully.

"Then Ronald,—Lewis Ronald?"

"Monsieur Lafitte might approve of his suit should he press it."

"He will, I know."

"Well, Mr. Robe, there is God and the Virgin and the saints, and there is I, to pray to them. You must trust me. I have accepted your confidence as you have given it. I don't know what my niece's nature may be. I hope it is not as mine was. I was a wild, wilful girl. Her mother was as different from me as a girl could be. But I will look after her, and the Church is strong in Louisiana. Monsieur Lafitte himself, though he defies the government, will not dare challenge it. As for her fancy,—whether it be yours or another's or St. Ursula's,—only God can decide."

She pushed her veil further back and looked at him intently.

"I can say no more on that subject. But there's another,—the war. We think about it,—we talk about it,—even in the convent.

War is wicked, brutal. Yet when two sides are striving in that way, a prayer may help, remember."

She bent her head and drew her veil, and her voice was broken.

"My father made war. Who knows more of it than I? And the day may come for New Orleans when the city shall be prayerful for its warriors,—a day not so far away."

"I shall have your good wishes then, and perhaps hers."

"Mine, yes, Captain Robe, and hers I know."

He thanked the nun for her good words and went outside the cool place into the brilliant sunshine; and he felt he was better, stronger for those few words. Besides Sister Madeleine, there was Philip Maurice in Virginia. It was not likely that Maurice would let Lafitte decide his own niece's future. But what reasons had Robe for feeling that Lafitte's course would be against Sallie Maurice's happiness? At least, he himself now could do no more; he would go at once to the general at Mobile.

He found Deschamps awaiting him with the same frivolous flow of talk he always had. But his jests now seemed stupid to Robe.

"How about Jean Lafitte?" he asked.

"Neither he nor Pierre is in the city. I can't get you word to him."

"No matter," said Robe, "and thank you much. No, I'm not sorry that I am going to leave your gayeties and your gambling. But don't forget the message to Mademoiselle de Renier."

"No," said Raoul. "Oh, there's your stupid friend, Cafferty."

Dennis, big, red-faced, shock-haired, came in.

"The governor gave his decision?" he asked.

"Don't you know it?"

"He has accepted our friend's proposal, and has advised General Jackson to do the same."

"The devil!" said Cafferty. "I mean it's an alliance with the devil."

Deschamps sat regarding the two and whistling a popular air.

"I wish your friends were not all these light-headed Frenchies," said Dennis angrily, but in a low voice. "Well, good luck to you." And he went out.

"What a brute of a fellow!" Raoul cried when he had gone. But Robe was thinking of Cafferty's strong wish to treat Barataria without mercy. "I am bound to state his side of the question to General Jackson," he said to himself.

When, some days later, Robe had made his report in full, the general's face seemed to become even more sallow and wrinkled and seamed; the bushy brows seemed to lower over the fierce, bright eyes; they seemed to be burning with the inner fire of a strong, passionate nature, of the inflexible will.

"I agree with Governor Claiborne in some respects. But we must wait and see. I'm not sure that we want to agree with the British in their overtures to robbers and pirates. Besides, they are now making an organization against the Baratarians. Let us wait to see what will happen."

"Yet he is sincere, general, this man Lafitte."

"He's trying to save himself, that's all," the general went on. "I can't stop the machinery of the Federal government."

Not long after, Robe, with the general, heard that the settlement of Barataria had been destroyed, and that only the Lafittes and a few followers had escaped. Commodore Patterson, Colonel Ross, the commandant at New Orleans, and Dennis Cafferty had been on this expedition. Robe understood Cafferty's feelings towards the Baratarians. What troubled him most was to know whether Miss Maurice had been there. And then one day he had this note:

"My dear Mr. Robe,—I write to let you know that my niece was with me when the expedition against Barataria took place.
"Sister Madeleine."

That was all; she said nothing of how Miss Maurice was, and yet Robe felt she had kept her promise to him. This was followed by a letter from Cafferty, who told him of the desolation that had been made in Barataria.* Governor Claiborne himself was angry at the turn of affairs, for he had felt himself bound to Jean Lafitte. But the governor had been overruled. Cafferty himself had thrown up his state commission and was enlisted with the United States troops. They had brought back to the city many prisoners and much booty.

Yet they had found no evidence that the Baratarians had been more than privateers save in one piece of jewelry which had belonged to a lady of New Orleans who had gone to sea seven years before, never to be heard from. And this was insufficient evidence; the jewel might have been obtained in many ways. "Still, I believe the worst of them," Cafferty went on. "But where Barataria was,—where we walked that day,—we left a wilderness. We took them entirely by surprise. They supposed we were down there to engage the British. I know you

---

* There are those who say that Lafitte's visit to Governor Claiborne was after the destruction of Barataria.—CORNELIA ROBE FENWOLD.

differ from me on this question, but it had to be done."

"You think a mistake has been made?" the general asked of Captain Robe. "They'll be back there."

"Yes, they'll be back there, but can we get them in our service?"

"We'll see, we'll see," the great Tennessean said.

In recording these events, now so long gone, Robe must state that he has not always followed current tradition and history. These things are written as his memory carried them. He does not agree with some of the accepted stories. And one word more here, before we go on to the more important part of the narrative, the names are often not the true ones, and Robe hopes that by no chance he has used for his substitutes any one ever really existent.

But the narrative must not pause for explanation. We have, awaiting us, the drama of Chalmette.

CHAPTER XII

THE ENTRANCE OF THE PRINCE

A WEARY man of iron, in frayed trousers, yellowed high boots, a flapping, shabby coat, old leather cap,—a thin, very erect figure, a hollow, wrinkled, sallow face, framed by a mat of iron-gray hair,—a face expressive of shrewd alertness, of a strong, decisive character,—such was he, as the well-known story goes, who, on the 2d of December, 1814, trotted up to the Spanish villa at the junction of the Bayou St. John and the Canal Carondelet, where a breakfast, such as the cooks had worked over, had been prepared for him. And the tired guest, sparing of his words,—Robe, who was of the general's escort, remembers,—asked only for hominy.

A certain lady took our captain aside.

"And this is he?—the general who is to defend us,—this"—her voice sank to contemptuousness—" this Kaintuck flatboatman ?"

"You should see him on another day," the aide said, diplomatically. "You will find him a man entirely different."

"Oh, I prepared this breakfast," quoth she, despairingly, and crossing her hands.

"Wait till to-morrow," Robe answered, smiling.

"A certain young lady has been asking for you," the lady went on. "I am about to censure Monsieur, our host,—ah, you understand French now,—for deceiving me with this General Jackson. But as for the young lady who has been inquiring so earnestly about you,—can't you fancy her name?"

"Ah, no," said Kit. "I have been among the fighting men."

"There are enough of them here. You will find the city all changed. Every man who can serve is in arms. Why, the prisoners are taken from the calaboose; and as for the blacks,—why, they never had so much fun. And Lafitte,—he is here from I don't know where,—he has been in hiding; but Captain Dominique You and Belouche are organizing the old band into two companies. And, then, there are men from Tennessee and all the parts of this country in all kinds of costumes. The city is a camp."

And this interesting lady went on with many little French expletives expressing her appreciation of the situation,—her surprise that the leader of all these assembled men was this strange backwoodsman, Andrew Jackson.

After this breakfast, the general, his tired face somewhat relaxed, rode to General Daniel Clarke's, where the governor, the mayor, and many others met him and looked him over suspiciously. But here a different person was shown. The general rose and made a very effective, if simply worded, speech.

"My friends, I am here to drive the enemy into the sea, or else to perish." And the interpreter passed the words on. And M. de St. Gëme turned to Robe,—"He's a man who makes you believe him."

In the midst of this entertainment a message was brought Captain Robe: "Mr. Jean Lafitte wishes to see the general." Robe went below, again astonished at the man's extraordinary daring.

Jean Lafitte was walking nervously up and down.

"You are here to offer your services?"

"Certainly, sir," Mr. Lafitte replied; "there's no attempt to disguise my presence here,—certainly."

"I regret," said Robe, "that Barataria has been destroyed. And where, pray, is your ward, Miss Maurice?—in Virginia, perhaps?"

"No, at Madame Demarche's plantation."

"You wish me to tell the general you are here?"

"Yes, captain," said Lafitte, calmly. "I am here to offer my services again. They certainly need them."

"Yes," Robe said; "I always have advised the acceptance of your offer. I agreed with Governor Claiborne."

"I have no fault to find with the governor. He has done as best he could," Jean Lafitte said.

"And Captain de Bertrand's granddaughter?" Robe asked again.

"No, Monsieur. She is now with my friend, Madame Demarche, as I told you."

"I will go to speak with the general," Robe said.

The general was now, with the animation of the occasion, quite a different person from him who, tired and looking it, had entered the city some hours before.

"The man Jean Lafitte is there," Robe said in a low voice.

"Eh, to see me?"

"To make you the same offer," Robe answered.

"I'll see him now," said the general, slowly; and he followed his aide out of the room, while that eager, critical crowd whispered about him. But already his strong words had carried a certain conviction. The creoles had begun to believe in him.

Robe shall always remember the meeting

between General Jackson and the leader of the Baratarians; Lafitte, courtly, handsome, with a knowledge of men; the other, homely, uncouth to a certain degree, yet with that same shrewd understanding of humanity and its foibles.

"Mr. Lafitte?" said the general.

"Yes, sir, Jean Lafitte, called the pirate, who is here to offer you five hundred fighting men, and in Captains Dominique You and Belouche two of the best artillery commanders in the world."

For five minutes the general seemed to hesitate, but at last he said:

"Your resolution is honorable, Mr. Lafitte. In the stress of these times, when I'm told that fifty sail of the British are putting up towards us, I accept, sir. Captain," he added, turning to Robe, "I will ask you to leave us."

Robe did not see Lafitte again that day; but when the general returned to General Clarke's reception-room, he paused to say in a low voice to his aide: "I admire your discrimination. He is the most remarkable man I have ever met."

As shortly after the general's carriage drew through the streets, the city seemed wild with enthusiasm. A great crowd rushed along, pushing, shouting plaudits in a half-dozen tongues,—a throng as strange and motley as you could imagine, that now held, by the impulse of its fervent nature, this lean, strong-faced man its preserver. And when they reached the headquarters this fervor knew no bounds. The flag had been unfurled and blew there, never to this date (1857) to be replaced by another, the flag of the United States.

The reception created a sort of response in that impulsive soul, the general. For, after all, he was a man of remarkable impulse, as Robe has observed is the case of many men who are styled geniuses.

There was at this occasion all of polite New Orleans, the women eager and chattering, the men not less inclined to criticise. To them entered a certain gravely self-held gentleman, a soldier in bearing, quietly mannered, and urbane to a nicety.

Robe felt a hand on his shoulder, and he turned about to see the young lady who had caused him so much sentimental trouble, Marie de Renier.

"Is that he? I thought he was a Kentucky flatboatman."

Robe, himself rather surprised at his chief's polite presence, said,—

"Why, yes, indeed; that is our general, Andrew Jackson."

"Well," said Mademoiselle, with one of her bewitching smiles, "he is a prince."

And this sentiment was repeated many times after dinner. "You were mistaken. You said a lean, gaunt man appeared,—a regular red Indian. Do you know what Marie de Renier says?—he is a prince." Which proves that, like most nervous men, General Jackson could change his demeanor under the spur of excitement.

But just then Mademoiselle was looking over her former conquest with a deal of attention, wondering, perhaps, if he would show any of the old symptoms of absorption in her entertaining self.

"You are thinner than you were," she announced at last.

After a moment she added,—

"I had your news from Raoul,—of whom you met at Barataria."

"The English lieutenant. You should hate 'em all," he retorted.

"Who says that I don't?" she said, with a nervous little laugh. "Ah, there is Louis Ronald. He has a company of his own. I saw him the other day, near Madame Demarche's, riding with a yellow-haired girl—very pretty, indeed—in black. He lied to me about Mr. Beaumont's engagement. I don't like him."

Robe looked across at the man, who apparently had done him so small injury, and yet whom he disliked so much. Would this fellow again act the tale-bearer? Would he carry news to Madame Demarche's guest that he had seen him talking with the pretty De Renier? Raoul came across the room to him, and he left Mademoiselle with a stiff bow across the room to Ronald. He forgot his surroundings. Was it not quite possible that the astute Lafitte intended to marry her to this powerful man, who stood for all that riches and position signified in New Orleans, for the power that Lafitte courted?

The next day the favor the general's second and third appearances had made and his bold words of perfect self-confidence had indeed reached through New Orleans. The city believed him with a great belief. French and Spanish joined in the zeal for the defence. Though the French had small liking for the American, they had a great dislike for England, and, if the Spanish were more lukewarm, they, too, were carried away by the contagious enthusiasm. Governor Claiborne had freed the prisoners in the calaboose, as has been said, many of whom were Lafitte's Baratarians. The captains, Dominique You and Belouche, were openly on the streets, as they had been, indeed, before Lafitte's interview with General Jackson. Lafitte himself was not to be found. It was said that he had gone to look up other of his Baratarians, who had been in hiding since the destruction of their retreat about Grand Terre. Robe had sought him out to make some further inquiries about Miss Maurice, but he failed to see him. When he called at the Ursulines for Sister Madeleine he found that she, too, was somewhere in the country,—they did not know exactly where. Yes, she had been at Madame Demarche's with her niece. And Robe, a very busy man in those days, went back to his duties. He saw the stern-faced Cafferty, who gave him more in particular the story of the desolation of Grand Terre, made now "a wilderness of wind-swept grasses and sinewy reeds, waving away from a thin beach, ever speckled with drift and decaying things, worm-riddled timbers and dead porpoises." *

And how may Robe describe the animation of the city? There were the blacks as well as the whites, companies of free men of color and of the black refugees from San Domingo who had stood by their white masters in the uprising there. There were the trim, constantly parading creole gentlemen, contrasted with the rough fellows making

---

* *Vide* Lafcadio Hearn. I have added it to my grandfather's description.—Cornelia Robe Fenwold.

CHALMETTE 167

General Coffee's famous " dirty shirts." There were Hinds's fine cavalrymen. There were the United States regulars, such as they were in 1814. There were the veterans of other days, formed into a home-guard. And we must not omit the Baratarians, with their red shirts and turbans and bold eyes, the admiration of all. The very servants, even Robe's Simon Wesley, burnished their masters' arms zealously, feeling they, too, were of the affair. And on the fortifications the slaves worked and sang, and held themselves quite important parts of the defence.

Yes, New Orleans took the occasion with Gallic ardor; nor must Kit omit the women, from ladies to servants, with snapping black eyes, who watched it all; the gay gossip, the tattle and flirtation of drawing-room and street. But there was one face that he didn't see at all; and he wondered about her, with a certain dull pain at his heart. When he saw his aversion, Ronald, he felt that same resentment. For he doubted not that he was often at the Demarche plantation, whence Kit's present duties kept him.

Now, one day—Kit believes it was the tenth—a messenger brought the news that as far as the glass could carry, in the water between Chandeleur and Cat Islands, were sails and sails. And what sails, indeed! The French Tonnant, captured in the Nile; the Royal Oak; the Ramillies; the Norge; the Bedford; the Asia; the Armida,—fifty sails, with a thousand guns; sailors who had carried Great Britain's flag triumphant in many and many a fight against the strongest foes in the world. And those vessels brought veterans of the Peninsula,—men who had burned Washington and ravaged Kit's own countryside. The messenger's report—soon enlarged from many sources—went on: Admiral Cochrane had already sent launches, with carronades and manned by a thousand men, sailors and soldiers, to drive the American flag from the lakes. And these were to be met by Lieutenant Catesby Jones's six gunboats and thirty-five guns! Perhaps they were fighting down there now.

The mercurial creole continued, dilating on the situation. What have we against such an armament? An army that didn't have many uniforms among them,—the creole fancy was serious over this matter of uniforms; Fort Philip, down the river, badly kept up; back of us the Spanish Fort,—pretty, to be sure, but what else? a few batteries more; the mud fort of Petites Coquilles. But General Jackson held his peace and said nothing; he had declared the city should not be taken; that was sufficient. Yet, you who know the present temper of New Orleans, imagine the chatter then, the lifting eyebrows, the brisk gesticulations.

Imagine Captain Robe meeting Mademoiselle de Renier of an afternoon, and Mademoiselle whipping a little silver dagger from her bodice.

"What does that mean?" he asked.

"I hear they have a toast," said the young lady, "'booty and beauty.' If they get here ——" Mademoiselle ended by brandishing her dagger. "I am not the only woman in New Orleans so equipped."

"What if it should be our friend, Mr. Beaumont?"

"I hate him," Mademoiselle cried. "I should rather love you," she added, with a blow from her eyes that made our captain the least embarrassed. Did she after all seriously remember his sentimental approaches? While he jested, he was troubled; and he heard Mademoiselle's light laughter behind him. What a vain creature is man; and how well the women know it!

As Kit pushed through the bustling street to his quarters, a hand suddenly caught his shoulder.

"Pardon, captain," said a familiar voice; and turning, he saw his Baratarian acquaintance, La Roux.

"This is for you, captain."

And he read:

"Take ten men, and have bearer lead you to Jean Lafitte, whose orders you are to obey,—using your discretion.   "JACKSON."

"Where shall I find you?" Robe asked, turning.

"I will follow you, captain. I will take you and your men to Mr. Lafitte's barges below the city."

CHAPTER XIII

AT MADAME DEMARCHE'S

THE two barges were close together. Lafitte's whiskered men bent low to their oars; Robe's followers, for the most part Tennesseeans, talking, and those who were not oarsmen nervously fingering their rifles; the low banks receding; the outlines of a gunboat of Commodore Patterson close under the opposite shore.

Lafitte was quiet and reserved, with now and then some word to La Roux. Robe had followed the general's orders literally, and now he had asked no question of the calm, handsome, self-poised man, who, criminal or no, commanded respect for his extraordinary ability, particularly in the way he avoided consequences. Perhaps Lafitte read his thoughts, for he turned to him suddenly with that affable smile which recalled to Robe the visit to Grand Terre.

"You know General Coffee? Yes, of course. At a reception he hesitated, but I went up to him,—'The pirate Lafitte,' I announced myself."

"He is a good commander for the men he has, this General Coffee," said Robe.

"So I wanted him to understand that I was conscious of my position," Lafitte said. "I never enjoyed patronage."

"You seem plainly enough in our service now," Robe answered.

"Well, possibly. They—my enemies—say I am profiting by the condition of things. I may be, Captain Robe."

And then he turned to give a direction in Spanish; he had a half-dozen languages at his tongue's end.

"Lieutenant Jones fought the enemy last night. It was musket to musket, cutlass to cutlass, and hand to hand. Jones cut into the open barges, sinking many. They say the waters were filled with red-coated men. But it ended——"

"They were driven back?" Robe asked.

"This news must just have reached the city."

"La Roux brought it to me,—to the general. They closed in on them, beating our crews back, and driving them below. By noon, captain, they held Lake Borgne. Is it an omen of the result? There are those who consider it may be."

For a moment Robe felt a suspicion of this ally. What if he should turn against them now? What if, after all, he had accepted the British overtures? What if, when it came to battle, the Baratarians should be foes in their midst? But Lafitte's keen eyes were on the Virginian's face, and he read his thoughts as easily as if he had spoken so many words.

"If it be so, that I am playing false, you will allow that I do it well," Lafitte said.

"I said nothing on that subject," said Robe, starting.

"I am not a child at understanding a man's thoughts, Captain Robe. And perhaps the best answer I may make is that I am here—you are here—to intercept that very business you think of. The English are at the Isle des Pois, where they suffer from the dews by day, the frosts by night,—where they are looking to the approaches to the city. They are deliberating on several plans proposed them."

" Proposed them,—through spies?"

" The Spanish fishermen and certain persons in the Spanish or English interest. La Roux, from sources we know of, has brought news that an English officer, disguised as a fisherman, is to meet a certain gentleman we know of at Madame Demarche's."

" I know of?—Ronald?" Robe asked, showing his own first surmise.

" No other; I trusted him. You dislike him," said Lafitte, watching him. " You have surmised it. Instinct isn't a bad guide at times. But I own I trusted him."

" Yet I thought there was not a creole traitor in Louisiana," the other said.

" He is partly an Englishman. He honestly believes that Louisiana would be better under English rule. He was disappointed that I refused the advances made to me.

Naturally a monarchist, he prefers England or Spain. He is sincere enough."

"He was interested in Barataria."

"Barataria, as Barataria, has ceased to exist. It is a matter now of the United States. I will confess that we—Dominique You, Belouche, and I—are fighting for social recognition. And we will have it. But we prefer it from the United States."

"Yet they burned your quarters, after the governor's acceptance of your offer, though the governor couldn't have prevented it."

"Don't you see, man," Lafitte said, frankly, "that it appears better for us to gain the recognition of a country which we know can't be conquered, which is nearest the operations on the Gulf?"

"That is the business proposition, broadly put," Robe agreed. "I agree with you that England can't make us colonies again. But as for this Ronald,—he is at Madame Demarche's?"

"Madame is his second cousin."

"And she knows of this?"

"Certainly not; but Ronald chose it as a

quiet place, where he easily could meet the British agent. There are many winding water-ways leading there from the mouth of the Pearl River. I am going there ostensibly to escort Madame to New Orleans. She says her neighbors, the Valleres, are not afraid. Why should she be? We will keep your men in reserve. We will reach the house by a way. I will inquire about Ronald. The British spies should be here this afternoon."

"Your ward, Miss Maurice, is there?"

"She insists that she should be here, though Mr. Maurice has twice sent for her to return to Virginia. He is her legal guardian. I am only an executor under Captain de Bertrand's will."

Lafitte watched Robe's face as he spoke of her. He did not deny that he had hoped to have her marry Ronald; he had not expected that Ronald had gone to the extreme of plotting that La Roux's advices indicated. His object in coming there was to get Ronald and the disguised officers from Admiral Cochrane, together with the Spanish fishermen who escorted them. His Baratarians were to beat about, with their useful knowledge of land and water, while he and Robe were to go openly to the house.

They carried this plan out in every detail, leaving the one barge with La Roux's half, of the Baratarians and Robe's men in a hidden spot, while the other went on much farther up the river, coming at last to rest under a thick hedge of yucca. Robe followed Lafitte to an out-building, where he gave a peculiar low whistle that did not penetrate far; but suddenly, from the corner of the house, a bent, white-haired and bearded negro appeared.

"Eh, M'sieur Lafitte," he cried, in that patois which Robe cannot attempt to render, though by this time he understood it fairly well. "Were the officers after M'sieur again?"

"Tell Henriette to let Madame know that Monsieur wishes to see Madame in the old way. Stay, is Monsieur Ronald about?"

Gabriel thought that Monsieur Ronald was walking somewhere with Mademioselle

Maurice; and nodding his head wisely, he turned away. Presently he returned, beckoning. They were shielded from observation along the little path by the thick, bare branches of a hedge, and at a door Henriette, the mulatto girl of Robe's former visit, awaited them. Henriette carefully had sent away the other servants. Gabriel, who was Henriette's father, guarded the farther end of the path. The girl broke into little exclamations of pleasure at seeing Monsieur Lafitte.

"Had the governor turned against Monsieur once more?" she asked, with the easy familiarity of a servant born to the household.

As she was speaking, Sallie Maurice rushed out, putting both her hands out to Lafitte.

"We are so glad to see you."

And then she noticed Robe, and turned to him rather coldly, he fancied.

"And you are here, Captain Robe?"

"I notice you have not returned to Virginia," he said, lamely.

"After the affair at Barataria my aunt felt it her duty to look after some who were hurt. They were men, though bad men, perhaps;

they had been my grandfather's people. I helped in what I could."

"They are free from the calaboose, Mademoiselle. They are soldiers of the United States."

Miss Maurice flushed, and she looked at Robe.

"They are pardoned?" she said.

"They are taken into the service," Robe answered, feeling her coldness. They had entered the room, Robe remembered, where Mrs. Claiborne and Lafitte had that play of wit and compliments. Perhaps Lafitte, too, remembered it, for he smiled.

"And Monsieur Ronald, my dear Mademoiselle Sallie? We heard he was sauntering with you."

"He will saunter no more with me, Monsieur, despite your wish."

"My wish may have changed," Lafitte said, with a meaning glance towards Robe. "Ah, Madame."

For Madame Demarche had entered, fresh and smiling.

"How you bring old New Orleans days

to me, Madame," Lafitte said; " evenings on balconies, gossip, dances——"

" Flirtation," said Madame. " Ah, yes, flirtation, and the subscription balls, to whom none was a more liberal subscriber than Monsieur Jean Lafitte," she added.

" Those days are gone, but in the period of my outlawry no one was kinder than a certain widow, whose husband had helped me much. She remembered, and now I am here insistent on your returning to New Orleans. The British will be here. You at Villere's and Demarche's and Chalmette's must leave for New Orleans,—you yourself, now, on my barge, which awaits you."

" We can't."

" I insist," he said.

" And when Lafitte insists," Madame retorted, " you obey. It's a proverb." And she courtesied, mockingly.

Lafitte whispered something. She grew suddenly pale.

" It can't be so."

" I know."

"Well, if you know." And she started. "We will obey Monsieur, Mademoiselle. We will put a few things together, and leave Henriette to follow with more. We go to the city at once. You will excuse us."

Sallie Maurice had been standing near Robe, but neither saying a word. For some reason his speech seemed to have deserted him. Now she bowed and followed Madame.

"You told her of Ronald?" he asked.

"I told her I believed there were English spies on her ground. I told her she must obey me."

"She believed you?"

"She never has had reason to doubt me," he said.

At the moment Madame and Miss Maurice entered, followed by Henriette with some luggage.

"You want everything to remain the same?" Madame said.

"Yes, no apparent change. I will receive him when he returns," Lafitte replied. "It's at the old landing, by the back path?"

"Yes," said Madame, "I leave the situation

to you. Au revoir, Monsieur Robe," and she gave Robe her hand.

"I dare say," Sallie said, "I may see you in New Orleans."

"You don't appear to wish to see me," he said.

But she ignored his remark; only extended her hand, and left them with yet a dash of red on her cheeks.

"Why do we remain?" Robe asked, turning to Lafitte.

"You will see presently."

At the moment there was a tapping on the door.

"La Roux."

"Yes, captain," said La Roux, entering.

"You saw it all?"

"Yes."

"How many were there?"

"Seven. Two were Englishmen gotten up like the others."

"You watched till after he had left them?"

"Yes, captain. Then, before they knew

it, we were down on them. There wasn't a cry."

"So they are safe in that glade?"

"Yes, certainly."

"And he should be here?"

"In five minutes."

"Madame will be embarked by that time. Do you, La Roux, take the other barge to the place where the prisoners are."

La Roux nodded and went out, eager, nervous, alert. Has Robe recorded that he was the only one of the Baratarians, save Jean Lafitte himself, who did not wear a beard; that he had a certain urbane, well-bred air, such as the Lafittes and Dominique You possessed in so remarkable a degree?

CHAPTER XIV

LAFITTE AND THE TRAITOR

It must have been, to show La Roux's accuracy, exactly five minutes after when Ronald, softly humming to himself, entered the house and turned towards the room where he doubtless expected to find his hostess or Miss Maurice. La Roux had anticipated him by taking a roundabout way, and he had walked slowly with his thoughts, little thinking that the two English officers whom he had just left were prisoners. As he entered, he stopped in amazement, looking from Lafitte to Robe.

"Oh, Monsieur Lafitte, this is the usual pleasure," he said. "You are always appearing,—disappearing again. You, too, are paying a visit to our old friend, Madame Demarche."

"No, and yes. I came to have Madame

go to the city. I have persuaded her. She has started by this time, I believe."

" Isn't this rather sudden ?"

" I have reason to believe that some of Admiral Cochrane's men may be here."

" What !" Ronald said, without moving a muscle,—" you believe that they know the water-ways ? It may be,—through the fishermen."

" Yes, and there are others as well. I intend to have the general send down a considerable force to watch the bayou and canal leading to this place."

" Have you any information ?"

" Some, some," Lafitte went on, like a cat playing with a mouse. " I didn't fully realize the danger till I was here myself. I could not believe my plain information that there was a Louisianian who might make an exact statement of the number of our forces, of the condition of the defences."

" Monsieur !" Ronald said, paling.

La Roux appeared.

" I have some papers, captain," he said.

" Bring them here."

Lafitte unfolded them.

"Back, La Roux," he said. "Ah, a map of every water-way about here,—an accurate map. Yes, and plans of the forts, such as they are."

Ronald looked from Lafitte to Robe, and then to La Roux. You could see that he understood the situation, and was considering his position. La Roux, though he had been told to return to his men, still hesitated.

"I have to report that one fellow ran. We couldn't get a fair shot at him. He jumped into the bayou and reached the bushes. We tried to follow him, but were caught in the marsh. He must have been swallowed up."

"Go, I tell you," Lafitte said, sternly. "Wait me there. I have an interview with Monsieur."

As La Roux went out, he said, as if meditating the force of every word:

"Monsieur Ronald, I rarely have been deceived in men."

"No, rarely," sneered the other; "that has

been the measure of your success, Monsieur."

"Yes," said Lafitte, slowly, "that may be. I even acknowledge it. But there's another matter. Monsieur, you owe some part of your income to our organization."

"Yes," said Ronald, looking at him without a tremor in his voice. "Yes, Monsieur Lafitte."

"You have said 'yes,'" Lafitte said. "May I add to my 'yes' that once I had occasion to shoot a man down,—nay, twice,—after I had taken the management of the affairs of Barataria."

He looked at Ronald for a moment as if critically. Robe, watching the two, like a spectator at a play, remembered the story of Grambo, the pirate, who, when Lafitte was completing his organization of the privateers and buccaneers of the Gulf, resisted the chief, who shot and killed him in the Great Temple, the place of their trade. And there were many other stories of like kind of this man, who now stood, strong and inflexible, the carelessness of his mannerisms gone, before this delinquent. For the first time Ronald started nervously, and his hand went involuntarily to his belt. Lafitte laughed with a fine scorn, not himself moving.

"Bring out your pistol, cocked and primed. I dare you to do it. For, deadshot though you may be, I don't think you can be quicker than I. For I judge you a mutineer, and the worst. For I trusted you, which I rarely do. There is some fine quality of pretence about you that made me. And you have deceived me. I supposed that you were following our policy,—to stand with the United States."

"A mistaken policy," said the other, sullenly. "You entered into it to secure your pardon, but what if England succeeds?—and she will, I know."

"And Monsieur Ronald's service will be remembered, and Jean Lafitte's refusal will be punished."

Ronald began to laugh, contemptuously, bitterly.

"Fool, this is another matter,—Admiral

CHALMETTE 189

Cochrane embarked sixteen hundred men in yesterday's rain. They will be here before you know. The rest will follow. How can Jackson resist them?"

"And I'll be confounded with this," said Lafitte, slowly. "You have given the information to the spy of the numbers, of the plans of the forts and the works, of the situation of the forces."

He spoke deliberately, as if considering the details of the situation carefully. Then he tore into bits the papers La Roux had brought from the English prisoners,—the plans Ronald had furnished them.

"If what you say may be true, at least they shall not have those papers," he said.

And then from under his coat he pulled two duelling pistols.

"I came prepared for this contingency," he said.

"What do you mean?" Ronald cried, while the single spectator watched like one fascinated.

"I am going to concede you the right of your opinion,—the right of a gentleman,—if as insubordinate to Barataria you should die. I give you a chance,—the duel,—a good chance, Monsieur, with your skill."

"I will not fight you, Lafitte. I refuse to fight you."

"Then, Monsieur, I must be simply the traitor's executioner. I will shoot you down."

For two moments Ronald deliberated. Perhaps he thought of springing away through the door, but he knew that Lafitte certainly would bring him down.

"Give me the pistol," he said at last, looking up grimly. He trusted to his skill, even against Lafitte.

Here Robe interrupted:

"This is an impossible situation," he remonstrated. "We have Mr. Ronald here as a prisoner. We must take him to New Orleans and deliver him to the authorities."

"Monsieur," Lafitte said, turning to him with a gleam of anger, "you will please to hold your tongue. The authorities may have a quarrel with Monsieur Ronald, but I have, too, my private one, which it is my privilege to settle."

"I grant you that privilege," said Ronald, calmly. And whatever Robe's dislike of him,—his firm belief that he had been making love to Sallie Maurice,—he still had to grant him the quality of bravery, of admirable sang-froid.

"You are to witness this is a duel," said Lafitte.

"Yes, you are the witness, Monsieur."

And Robe, awed by something in both men's manner,—and himself brought up to respect the *code d'honneur*,—said,—

"If you both wish it, I can but agree."

And then suddenly fear seized him. What if this Ronald should kill Lafitte? How could he repeat the case to his general? And he felt certain that in that case he should return to the city alone, as he could not protect Ronald from the vengeance of the Baratarians.

"Yet I believe you are wrong, Mr. Lafitte," he added.

"That is my matter; you have agreed. Stand by your word," Lafitte retorted.

"It is here, then,—in this room?" Ronald asked.

"Yes, here."

"I don't care to see the other pistol. I can trust you, Monsieur Lafitte."

"Thank you, Monsieur," Lafitte said, ironically. "You will please say, calmly, 'One, two, three,' Captain Robe. On the three, Monsieur Ronald."

"On the three, Monsieur Lafitte," Ronald assented.

Robe in his day has witnessed some duels; and he is glad to notice that the practice in these later years is going out of repute, even in the South. He has heard many duelling stories, from that of Sheridan's by candle-light in the London tavern to the one between Mr. Hamilton and Mr. Burr, which excited so much feeling. He has had several friends killed on the field, among others the brave Captain Decatur. But in his own experience, or in any of these stories, there surely was never anything more impressive than this duel between Lafitte and Ronald, in a room which he associated with women's light talk,—where the laughter of Mrs. Claiborne and Madame Demarche and the presence of Sallie Maurice still seemed to linger.

"One," he said, fearfully; "two," after the pause.

The pistols were levelled and the two men looked straight into each other's eyes,— "three."

The flash came; Ronald tottered: the report rang; Ronald's arms flew out, with a rush of blood from his mouth, and he fell in a heap.

"I have done my duty," Lafitte said, grimly, putting his smoking pistol on the table.

At the moment a red uniform was projected into the doorway, with a crowd of others behind.

"You are prisoners," came a stout English voice. "The house is surrounded. What's this?—a murder?" he added, in some dismay.

"He brought you here," said Lafitte, turning calmly to the officer. "The informer, sir, has been executed, but he had a chance of his life. It was a duel."

"He cannot answer," said the lieutenant, leaning over the prostrate Ronald; "he is dead."

Robe's eyes followed Lafitte's to the little fragments of paper on the floor; the informer was dead; the maps and details he had furnished were destroyed. Lafitte stepped over to him and whispered: "If they had taken La Roux, we should have heard firing. La Roux has gotten away, or is in hiding with the spies and their crew."

Robe never saw this strange man so excellent as in this expression of his belief that he had outmanœuvred the man he had killed. He, too, seemed to have no regret for his deed.

"No more words," said the officer, harshly. "Seize them, sergeant."

Four scarlet-coated men walked over to the prisoners, as a grim-featured sergeant directed.

"We have these two, Mr. Berden," said the sergeant. "But that major over there and the other man * jumped out of the window and reached the woods."

Then the prisoners knew that the Villeré as well as the Demarche house had been surrounded, that the family there had been taken, but that Major Villeré and another person had made a bold dash for liberty,— for the chance to warn the city, which was but eight miles away. Lafitte's usually noncommittal face betrayed a smile of some self-satisfaction.

"Take the prisoners to the general," the lieutenant said, brusquely, "and I'll finish the search of the premises and look at the dead man."

"It was a duel," said Robe here. "I am the witness."

"That's to be decided," the lieutenant answered; and then, noting the quality of his prisoners, he added, "You'll state the circumstances to General Keane, who doubtless will wish to put some questions to you."

---

* *Vide* a short story of the author's in *Youth's Companion*, "How New Orleans was Saved."

As they were brought outside, Robe reflected again that while the secret information obtained from the Spanish fishermen or others,—perhaps from the dead Ronald,—had brought the enemy so near the city, they at least did not seem to have La Roux. Yet he remembered that even in the excitement of the last moment of the duel he had heard some rapid shots. Lafitte himself had been oblivious to the sounds. Then La Roux, after all, might be taken. Yet, remembering that Major Villeré and some one else, from the sergeant's word to his superior, had made a bold dash for freedom, there was the chance that the shots might be from their pursuers. And even if La Roux and his men were taken, their two English prisoners and their Spanish fishermen crew could not produce the plans which Lafitte through sagacious foresight had destroyed. It was evident, now, that the spies had been sent ahead to confer with Ronald, who doubtless wished to return unobserved to New Orleans, to continue his supply of information.

These thoughts, which can be put here

better to explain the situation, ran through Robe's mind almost in the few seconds before they reached the lawn outside the house. And all the fields,—back to the orange groves,—seemed to be dotted with red-coated men, who were moving along the road on the levee to the upper side of the plantation, where they seemed to be forming, as it proved afterwards, in three columns. And as the two prisoners were brought into the grounds immediately about the Villeré manor a small battery was being thrown up. Here, as at Madame Demarche's, were frightened, chattering crowds of blacks under guard.

The surprise of both plantations had been the most decided possible; and the invaders seemed to be making the most of their few moments' occupancy. Robe's heart sank. They certainly would push on to the unprepared city. This doubtless was the van, now waiting for the main body.

The day, as the histories state and Robe remembers, was December 23, 1814.

CHAPTER XV
THE ESCAPE

They were brought into a room where a stout, white-haired man, in plain clothes, was consulting with a taller, black-bearded, uniformed young man. The former was Sir Alexander Cochrane; the latter, General Keane.

The sergeant briefly stated the circumstances under which the prisoners had been taken.

"A murder?" General Keane asked.

"No, sir," Lafitte interrupted,—"a duel. The man was a Louisianian proprietor who was a spy in our midst."

"I dare say you call every man a spy who is dissatisfied with Yankee misgovernment," the admiral remarked. "This will be looked into."

"You may know his name," Lafitte said,—"one Ronald."

CHALMETTE

"He!" General Keane exclaimed.

"As I thought,—as I knew,—having other certain proofs," Lafitte said. "You may like to know, too, that I, who killed this fellow, am Lafitte, whom you once approached."

Sir Alexander Cochrane wheeled about.

"You are Lafitte, the pirate? You are the outlaw who preferred their side to our protection?"

"I am Lafitte, the pirate."

"And this gentleman?"

"Christopher Robe, captain in the United States army," Robe answered.

"And you two deliberately killed this man without process of law?"

"'Twas, Sir Alexander, through the court of the duel."

"Well, well, we can't discuss that now, as I have said. D'ye mind telling me how much of a force Jackson has?"

"Not in the least, general," Lafitte replied; "twelve thousand men in the city, and four thousand at English Turn."

Now it had happened that a detail on a

reconnoissance had taken four American pickets at the entrance of that bayou, which had brought the English van to the canal and Villeré's. And by the merest chance—the most extraordinary coincidence—these persons, one a creole gentleman of standing, had stated that General Jackson's force was twelve thousand in the city, and four thousand at English Turn. So now the admiral and the general exchanged glances. And this coincidence, in fact, saved New Orleans. For General Keane, believing that statements from such different sources must be worthy of belief, did not dare venture farther till he should be strengthened by his complete force. After some further cross-questioning the sergeant was ordered to take the prisoners to a cotton-house which had been selected as a guard-house. After the escape of the two gentlemen from the manor itself the British officers perhaps were not minded to take a further risk there; or, rather, it seemed fit to herd these two with the common prisoners.

This house stood at a field's edge, with

CHALMETTE

close behind it thick trees and shrubs, cypresses, palmettoes, vines, cane-brakes, a dense tangle descending into a stretch of impassable morass, so far as the British could perceive in their brief occupancy of the place. The worn path to the cotton-house edged this thick growth, and no sentinels had yet been stationed on that side.

When, about half-way from the manor to the cotton-house, the sergeant and the guards with the prisoners were at a point where the path came nearest the thickly wooded morass, there was a quick crack of rifles. The aim was unerring; three men fell. Lafitte brought the sergeant down with a blow of the fist, and catching Robe by the shoulder, he said, "That fool, La Roux!" and sprang straight into the bushes. There was a narrow opening before, with here and there broad stretches of water. Shouts and cries followed. Robe was at Lafitte's heels, springing from mound to mound. The tangle would have been inextricable save to the trained sense which had followed it many times. By this way

Lafitte had reached his friend, Madame Demarche, on many a day. And now, as he sprang forward, he knew unerringly which mound to take, turning about to warn Robe to follow him carefully or else he would sink in a soft, devouring soil. Behind them there gathered a half-dozen alert figures of those who had been stationed by the keen La Roux at that point. He had watched the enemy from his hiding; had seen the selection of the cotton-house for a guard-house; had surmised shrewdly that the two prisoners would be brought that way. And now the cries sank behind them. The soldiers, not knowing where the footholds were, struggled in what seemed a quicksand, and shortly the fugitives had put half a mile between themselves and their pursuers. Over a similar way Major Villeré had fled, after hiding in the lucky cypress, of which more later.

At last they came to a narrow stretch of clear water,—perhaps ten feet wide,—where to a secure bank the barge was moored.

"When you told me, captain, to keep the barge in hiding, I brought it here."

"Good, La Roux. You said one fellow escaped you in the capture. They might have looked for you in the other place."

"Yes, I thought that, captain."

Lafitte scanned the barge-load, Robe's Tennesseeans' sharp faces watching them; the sullen faces of the Spanish fishermen; the two others, one dark, one fair, of the young Englishmen who had ventured to meet Ronald. Lafitte smiled grimly.

"Your men are very near the city, you may like to know. Your luck has been bad."

"Yes," said one, the fair-haired boy, who looked the gentleman, despite rough clothes; "but we are prisoners. Still, we shall not be so long."

"When Admiral Cochrane shall dine in New Orleans," Lafitte said, mockingly. "On, La Roux. This will bring us out four miles below the city."

The barge was started, the Baratarians gleefully whispering over the rescue, the prisoners moodily silent.

"You're a fool, La Roux!" Lafitte cried, with a burst of rage, his eyes flashing.

"Yes, my captain," said La Roux.

"You should have gone on and warned the city."

"And let the English hang you, my captain?"

"They would have hung the pirate," Lafitte said, as if reflectively; and he said no more to La Roux.

And so silently, save for the oar-dip, they wound through a mysterious labyrinth and suddenly on to the river. Robe's thoughts went over the exciting events of that day; he could hear Miss Maurice's voice, see her eyes. She, at least, was safe by Lafitte's foresight. And then he remembered the episode of Ronald, that duel, the interruption, the strange chance of the success of La Roux's shrewd calculation. It was obvious that now the morass would be defended in some way, or else that guard-house abandoned.

As they neared the city the cathedral bell was tolling out over the waters and the distances.

"They know!" said Robe.

"Villeré reached here," Lafitte said, laconically.

Leaving La Roux to look to the prisoners, Lafitte and Robe sprang ashore and ran towards head-quarters. The streets presented the most animated appearance possible,—men rushing to and fro, women calling down from balconies,—a kaleidoscope of color and activity.

As they came into the room they heard the general's voice.

"Gentlemen," he said, "the British are below; we must fight them to-night."

In the background stood Major Villeré, much torn and bedraggled.

CHAPTER XVI

THE BALCONY AT MADAME DEMARCHE'S

W*HAT* Lafitte said to the general,—whether, indeed, he explained Ronald's death,—is unknown to Robe. But,—trust to Jean Lafitte to defend his own position, whatever that might be,—General Jackson was deep in talk with the leader of the Baratarians. And in that critical moment the general was not inclined to question too closely ways and means. An army he wanted, an army he must have, and a part of it this Lafitte could supply.

Robe, indeed, had no time to consider the general's talk with Lafitte. For orders were passed swiftly; every aide was in requisition;—to Bayou Saint John for Planché's battalion, to the intrepid Coffee's detachment, to Gentilly for the battalion of blacks. 'Twas a galloping and a rushing through thronged streets. Songs joined the cries, and they shouted, at their lungs' best, "La Chant du Depart," "La Marseillaise," and "Yankee Doodle." In these piping times of peace you can't imagine such a scene, the color of it, the excitement of it.* It was fine, and great, and tremendous, as I find those adjectives used in a college essay of my grandson.

But here Robe must pause to tell of how he saw Major Villeré. The story of how the news was brought to New Orleans is not complete without this addition. He jumped from the window, you remember, after the enemy had surrounded his house, gained the woods and the swamp,—the same where La Roux made the *coup d'état* of the escape. But in his case they succeeded in keeping him close in view. So that, closely pushed, he climbed a cypress and lay hid there till suddenly he heard a whining below, and looking down he saw a favorite setter that had followed him. There was but one thing to do; he descended and killed the dog,—his

---

* As I have written, my grandfather died before the Rebellion. We in Virginia were to know war in its most terrible aspects.— C. R. F.

good friend. As he told this story tears were in the brave gentleman's eyes. 'Twas like the death of a human being; and, as another has said, not the least of the sacrifices of those times was that poor setter's, who was given to save New Orleans. For the major reached the city, bringing the first warning, —since the other gentlemen and we were much behind him.

In those busy moments Robe snatched the time to visit Demarche's city house. He had looked to see Madame or Miss Maurice or Sister Madeleine among the crowds of the ladies on the balconies, who were watching the scene with animated interest. From a balcony Mademoiselle de Renier had called to him:

"You will soon be marching, captain," she said. "Ah, we are working so hard, preparing lint and bandages."

"You expect all to be killed?" he said.

"We shall care for you if you are only wounded; we will weep for you if you are killed," said Mademoiselle, gayly, yet with a touch of seriousness in her sparkling dark eyes. "But what shall we do if they attack us?"

"That will be, the general said, over our dead bodies. And as for you, Mademoiselle, there's, I'll repeat, that Mr. Beaumont I met at Barataria."

"Ah, you would tease," said she. "I met this morning a friend of the Demarches, and she was inquiring about you, Monsieur. I have my side of the argument."

"And where may Madame Demarche's be?"

"I knew you would ask that question," she cried,—"I knew it well. Go there, false one," she went on, with mock solemnity. "You see the house yonder through the trees."

"Adieu, Mademoiselle."

"It shall be au revoir," said she, pouting; "for you will come back and the bands shall play."

Robe bowed himself away, and then was rushing over to see the ladies Lafitte had sent from the plantation. He thought over his long past acquaintance with Miss Maurice;

how little he could have imagined her relation to these men whom the necessity of war had brought again into the pale of the law. He thought of the seeming incongruity of this young lady, conventionally bred, being brought into the fierce life of these buccaneers; of how she had come to New Orleans to her grandsire's death-bed; of how she had seen those things which were for strong men. She at least had not seen Jean Lafitte's vengeance on Ronald. She had been spared that. And yet, now all the horrors of war might be brought to her,—as to the city. As he had these thoughts, he remembered by contrast the old, quiet Virginian days,—the girl who was ever ready for a ride or a dance, who responded readily and mischievously to light frivolity. Had all these contrasted experiences changed her entirely? Was she that same young girl, or, oh, so different? Had impassable barriers been raised between them? He remembered with a certain satisfaction—in the very midst of his gloom—that she had twitted him over his attentions to little Mademoiselle de Renier; and then again how she had said, "The pirate's granddaughter." Yet even if she were of the blood of that mysterious, that terrible old man, she was as far above Robe as the stars above the earth. John Robe might have talked about the bad blood to his nephew. It was she,—not her blood,—who held the nephew's attention that moment as he walked through the eager, struggling crowd to Madame Demarche's. And there something surprised him; something put his heart to beating, for a voice called down:

"Ah, Kit, I thought you were going to forget us,—to leave us for the war without saying good-bye."

She was leaning over towards him with the old laughter in her face, the girlishness in her eyes.

"Yes, it would have been very ungracious of you," said Madame, looking him over with her shrewd, kindly eyes, "when it is our battle. We hear we left Demarche just in time; that they came down on us and on Villeré's and Chalmette's. Mr. Lafitte's and your escape was fine, indeed, and Major Villeré has just been telling us how he managed to bring the news. He says all the time he was a prisoner in the room he kept repeating: 'They will say that I showed the British the bayou and the canal leading here, because I am a creole dissatisfied with American rule.' Then he took the risk and succeeded in getting away. You never are sure of your neighbors,—that they may do brave things in an emergency."

Robe thought of that other whom they had left at Demarche's; that other who had done what Villeré had feared would be said he had done. Did they know of that? But Madame went on, turning grave:

"War has been brought home to us. Ah, how many more shall we hear of in these next days! Louis Ronald, they say, was killed."

"Yes," said Robe, looking anxiously at the Virginia girl; and perhaps she, too, was a little paler. The black she wore brought out her fairness, which she had from the Maurices. And he added to Madame,

"You know?"

"Mr. Lafitte has been here and told us."

How could he have told of that? and Robe felt himself shuddering. How could he have said, "I killed that man because he was a traitor,—killed him, indeed, when he had an equal chance of life in a fair duel,—but killed him? I had trusted him thoroughly, and suddenly found my trust in the wrong." Yet Robe was not squeamish about the duel, he has stated again and again; nor was the proceeding out of keeping with Lafitte's stern character, developed by his command of his lawless followers,—a command which had made him in many respects a great captain.

"It shocked us," Madame went on. "Mr. Lafitte did not tell us the particulars."

Ah, Lafitte had not told then! For a moment he was silent. He could not tell. Lafitte had preferred not to tell,—that was certain. He personally had no quarrel with Lafitte, with whom he had acted in his own official capacity,—that was all; save dislike in one particular: Lafitte's wish,—which he suspected had been to marry Miss Maurice to Ronald.

"It was one of the events of war," he said, non-committally.

"I never liked that man," Miss Maurice said, slowly. He looked at her quickly. Had she said that for his benefit?

"You saw much of him?" he asked. "You knew him very well?"

"No, not very well, to be sure. I might have changed my mind. It is terrible,—to think of him as dead. When I came to New Orleans I stopped over with my aunt. He came there with Mr. Lafitte."

"I had a note from you then," he said, smiling, telling it over again.

"Yes, yes," she said, flushing; "it was a silly little note."

"But I rather liked it," he retorted.

"There's no accounting for tastes, Kit. I shouldn't say that; the young lady is very pretty; I can account for it readily." And she smiled at him as he had not seen her smile since he had left her at Westmore.

"Oh, that isn't fair," he cried. "I could say those things of you,—if I wanted to. You know well enough."

"Could you?" she said. "Could you,—about poor Mr. Ronald, perhaps? I saw him in Barataria three times; in New Orleans once; at the plantation twice. He at least was always very nice,—though I didn't like him particularly, as I said before."

Madame was watching the two; perhaps drawing her own conclusions; she looked very serious; perhaps her thoughts were in other days,—when she had been on a balcony talking with some young gentleman; when certain expressions of the eye, of face, certain words, signified, indeed, a deal. Perhaps she was thinking of Ronald, whose family had been connected with hers,—whom she had known always; perhaps it was the fear that—with all the confidence General Jackson's assurances had gained—held New Orleans on that day. We might hope for the best; we might laugh and pretend to be brave, but who could tell of the morrow? The British sailors and soldiers had done so much; had known so much of the discipline of action. Now she rose and left them there on the balcony,—a balcony Robe always held after a dear, sacred place.

For some moments they were silent, and then the girl said, looking down,—

"Ah, Kit, you must understand me,—I shall think of you in your danger. I shall pray for you, as the nuns of the Ursulines will pray for the success of you all. I can't forget, this fearful day, that we played together."

"And that is all," he said. "Is it all? Be frank this last day. I thought of you,— with gladness and despair, too,—when I found that note you sent."

"Ah," she said, "you thought me jealous."

"Now, weren't you? Please to let me believe that you were, and I never can thank you enough,—never, dear. No,—not a word, not an objection."

"But," she said, pushing him away, "I am De Bertrand's granddaughter, and you———"

"And who were my people some generations back? Were they much better? Don't most of the English families date from rough, strong old fellows, who did exactly as Captain de Bertrand? And what, indeed, is it to you and to me? You are you, dear. And I,—I am a poor, weak chap, whose single virtue is that he knows who the nicest girl in the world is, and that he will try to deserve her."

When you were in love, did you make a speech like that? Did not the world seem a finer, better, grander place,—just for her? And if you have not lost the illusion, still, isn't it so through her? And, after all,—for all the pessimists,—honesty and truth and simple love are what make the world worth while. With any two of them we can see God; without them He sometimes may seem an impossibility.

Now Robe said,—and you can fancy how far he had progressed,—

"Tell me truly, Sallie. Was it so much the thought of your mother's family———"

"It was a very good family," she said. "My grandfather, from the way he was found,—do you know the story?—showed every evidence of gentle birth. My mother was well bred and educated. My aunt you know."

"I know her, and she was kind to me."

"She likes you," Sallie said, "because she knew I did."

"But tell me," Robe insisted, "it was not so much the thought of your grandfather's career as———"

"It was a fearful career," she said; "but, Kit, he was born in it,—brought up to it———"

"Yes, yes. But it was principally jealousy of Mademoiselle de Renier which made you refuse me."

"You are odious," she said,—"just odious."

"Well, that letter raised my hopes, and when you saved me from Belouche's crew———"

"It was Dominique You," she said. "It was but common humanity on my part. I have explained before. I think you are vain———"

"I am a bit," he acknowledged. "You have made me so. But you will make me vainer and braver by that acknowledgment."

"Why, Kit, I never heard of anybody so —vain. But,—but,—you are going away,—

perhaps to the wars. I don't care,—what you may be, dear, and,—yes, it was."

But that scene is not too much to be written about; Robe has recorded that balcony corner is ever to be held dear,—sacred. And all this had taken place in much less time than its telling; for Robe was but a little time out of the street, with its forming troops. And now he was hurrying to his duty with the feeling of her lips still on his; of her arms about him; of the delicious self-surrender that made her ever the one woman. Nor has he since changed in that opinion.

As he passed out Madame met him, and she saw it in his eyes. And she, too, smiled, and she took his hand.

"I congratulate you, my friend. But,— you did not tell her of Ronald?"

"You know, then?" he asked, suddenly turned sober.

"That Jean Lafitte killed him in a duel," she said. "Yes, he told me."

"And he did not wish her to know?"

Suddenly, for all his lover's mood, jealousy shadowed him.

"You think she fancied him?—ah, but I see, it is Jean Lafitte who doesn't wish her to know."

"He still has her property," Madame said. "And after her experiences in Barataria,—and since her grandfather was a violent man,—he thinks it as well that she should not know."

"Yes,—yes, he wants her good opinion,—he fears her bad one."

"He cares much for her, Monsieur."

"I am not afraid of him,—or the whole world, Madame. Yet it is good of you to tell me this. And you are his friend——"

"Yes, always his friend; but Mademoiselle Maurice has attracted me singularly. So I have told you. He would be a particularly bad man to thwart you. He doesn't like you any too well."

"Then why doesn't he show it."

"Perhaps he is too subtle; perhaps he might wish to please her. Her uncle in Virginia, Monsieur Maurice, will be down here,—after the peace. I shall feel easier when Monsieur Lafitte turns over the property. Not that he isn't quite trustworthy,—no, not in the least; believe me, I didn't imply that. Outside of the conduct and the interest of his trade, never was a man more trustworthy, Monsieur. He is trustworthy in his accounting to others. You know how well he is esteemed in New Orleans,—notwithstanding that trade; how heavily he contributes to the charities; how fine a man he is. But when he is thwarted,—when his passion is aroused,—he is a different man. Oh, you know. Well, it's this: I found him talking to me about arranging a marriage between her and Ronald, because that would bring together two fortunes acquired from the Gulf trade,—Ronald's through its Louisianian connection, to be sure,—but still in that way. This would continue his use of the two fortunes,—this would help his own influence in New Orleans. But suddenly I found him giving up that idea."

"Perhaps he already distrusted Ronald?"

"Never, till that discovery. And how much was his duel with Ronald caused by a quickly gained dislike of him in the condition of suitor?"

"She did not encourage him,—Ronald?"

"No, no, no; not in the least, Captain Robe. But I thought I would tell you. Jean Lafitte is such a strange man,—such a fearful man; so attractive, so unrelenting. My husband was his friend; he has been mine ever. Yet now,—Mademoiselle Maurice has seemed to me so much like a daughter,—a daughter I never have had,—that I don't want her hurt; and I thought I would tell you."

"Thank you, Madame. Monsieur Lafitte has been kindness itself,—as you have, indeed; and I am not afraid of him,—in the very least."

"Well, well, forgive an old woman's fancies, Monsieur, and good fortune to you,—and to the battle."

A low voice called from the balcony. He looked up to catch one last glimpse of her,—the particular her. She waved back to him, and her eyes reached to his heart.

Some moments after he ran across M. Deschamps and his friend, M. St. Gême.

"You look surprisingly good-natured," said Deschamps.

"You have the smile one should carry into battle," said St. Gême. And then the two creole gentlemen fell to their places in a fine body of men, straight, lithe, bearing themselves like soldiers,—the creoles! And there were Beale's rifles in blue hunting-shirts,—good shots all,—their weapons over their shoulders. And there were Hinds's cavalry. Then came General Coffee's command, a throng of uncouth, unshaven, long-haired men, wearing discolored hunting-shirts, coonskin caps, knives and tomahawks in their belts,—men who had taken their mannerisms from the Indians themselves. And then were the freemen of color, with behind them a hundred Choctaws in war-paint; and last the regulars.

Robe saw these in review beside the general, whom he joined at the gate of Fort Saint Charles. Then, after the schooner "Carolina," Commodore Patterson, began to move with the current, the general put his horse to the canter, followed close by his aides.

So the army of defence marched to meet those most efficient and distinguished troops, —whose van, if not much more, now awaited them about Villeré's and Chalmette's, and the fronts of the bayous and canals.

CHAPTER XVII

THE FIRST DAYS OF THE BATTLE

What is a man's impression of the days of a great battle and their intense activity? Robe, in recollecting it, hardly knows at all. He had been under fire several times, and he has recorded Lundy's Lane in these pages. The aide's sense of his own duties are rather in confusion. He remembers Hind's dragoons riding out, and turning back after some moments under a brisk volley from the British rifles. He remembers rushing about on various errands; he remembers the marshalling along the Rodriguez Canal, perhaps two miles from the enemy. And then there was the long wait, and the darkness rising and enveloping the enemy's lines, where the fires made sharp points of flickering light. An object was stealing down the river, though the enemy did not seem to be clear about it, —Commodore Patterson's "Carolina." And then there rang out—it had all fallen still—a strong voice over the waters and fields,—"Give them this for the honor of America," and there were points and lines of dancing lights and a persistent thundering.

Robe had been on an order to General Coffee, whose men were skirting the swamp at the right, awaiting these sounds that came sweeping over the levees and the fields. The general wished to delay a bit, and there must have been an hour before there began an irregular firing; when to all was a fearsome, human screech and a rushing together of dim figures, who, when they failed to fire because of the short distance, clubbed their muskets, man to man; the Tennesseeans drawing knives and brandishing tomahawks, which the prisoners taken called a most barbarous method of fighting, as perhaps it was. At the firing distance the superiority of the long American bore over the short English musket was proven that night of the exciting noises. For the "Carolina" kept up its angry fusillades, to which was added this *staccato* of firing. But before the struggle was at its heat Robe was back at the left with his general. Yet he knew the story as well as those who were in the hottest of it. 'Twas, to be sure, a most irregular, guerilla fighting, from the point of view of those trained British, but it gave that night the key of the fight,—the skill of American riflemen and gunners. For the British, ordered behind the levee to avoid the " Carolina's" fire, had sallied out to support their pickets and had been borne back. And when the second division came up the " Carolina's" firing still made the numbers not so unequal.

The scene blurred; in vague, scurrying outlines the winter swamp-fog swept over it, making the fires dull, uncertain, and gradually silencing the fighters.

A number of prisoners were taken, and among them an officer of the Ninety-fifth Rifles, who, on Robe's asking if anything could be done for him, replied, " Return General Jackson my compliments, and say that, as my baggage will reach me in a few days, I shall be able to dispense with his polite attentions." And, indeed, though we had been successful in that first night's sortie, it looked as if this proud British officer might be entirely in the right. 'Twas to him that Mademoiselle de Renier remarked, "I'd rather be the wife of a *Tennesseean*, roughly clad as he is, than a countess." And Mademoiselle's eyes flashed finely as she delivered that tribute to the good fighters who had marched fifteen hundred miles to be with Jackson at New Orleans.

But to return to the narrative. The next day was the twenty-fourth, and, as the late dawn came, the "Louisiana," new in the position, joined the "Carolina" in the bombardment of the camp. We on our side had been working with pick and spade making a line of defence off the bank of the Rodriguez Canal, taking anything we could put our hands on,—bits of timber, rails, and some cotton-bales, though very few of the latter were used, contrary to the story. The general had sent to the city the night before for picks and shovels, and nearly every man was at this labor, including the aides.

And so the twenty-fourth passed, and the

next night, a frosty, damp night, the ground cold and moist, leaving even our hardy men shivering, and greatly depressing the enemy, who imagined us five times as strong as we were. But on Christmas morning we heard from a spy that Lord Longford's now famous son, Sir Edward Pakenham, had arrived,—a general who had led the storming at Badajoz, and had been knighted for the charge at Salamanca. As the general urged his men to further endeavors with their spades and picks, he let drop the first and last expression of fear that Robe heard from his lips during those eventful days.

He was sitting at a table in the Macarty House (which he had taken for head-quarters), when Robe heard him say to General Coffee,—

"They may beat us. How can we hold out against soldiers like that?" Then his thin, pale, tired face lit with a smile. "But I guess we'll hold out, Coffee." What General Coffee said Robe did not hear. But Raoul Deschamps told our captain of a report to the effect that if Sir Edward should win, he was to be made Earl of Louisiana, which would have been a very proper title for so brave and notable a success.

The next day the firing was kept up from the gunboats, but was intermittent from our lines, we being for the most at our ditch; yet we noted that a great battery was being put on the levee, and by the next day those guns broke out on Commodore Patterson's vessels, tearing and rending, till suddenly there was a burst of flame and a tremendous report. The "Carolina" had blown up, and it seemed as if the "Louisiana" would share her sister vessel's fate; by towing she reached a point opposite our camp, when the crew and the men in the works began a cheer, which was echoed from the crowds of observers on the banks. For people came from the city and the surrounding country to see the struggle, as if it were some theatrical display.

"They are moving forward," said the general, who stood, telescope in hand, watching the enemy, "in two columns. Have Captain Dominique You bring a battery to command the road."

Further orders were passed to cut the levee, to bring forward the infantry, to have the crew of the "Carolina" take charge of one battery.

Robe found Captain You busied in his position, a score of red-shirted, grimy, and mud-stained followers about him. The aide pointed out the position he was directed to take. The captain shouted an order in French and Spanish.

"Eh, Captain Robe," said a voice over his shoulder, and turning he saw Jean Lafitte,— not the urbane Jean Lafitte, but the dangerous one.

CHAPTER XVIII

THE RIVALS

"You saw Mademoiselle," said he, slowly. And Robe, watching him with a sudden dislike, remembered what Madame Demarche had said.

"Yes, Monsieur Lafitte. And she will be my wife,—if I live through this."

"Is that your decision?" Lafitte said, with a perceptible sneer. His fine manners were gone; he was a bit begrimed, like his men. Now Robe and he stood near the gunners, in earnest rivalry.

"Monsieur," said Lafitte, when Robe did not answer, "I tell you frankly that I shall try to prevent this,—yes, I,—understand me, Monsieur."

"And why," Robe asked, "if I have her wish?"

"Because——"

And suddenly Lafitte's voice broke into passion,—

"I am not a man to be trifled with, Captain Robe. And I'll tell you what I mean. Why didn't I give my hand to those yonder?"

He pointed to the British line.

"Because," he went on, "there had come into my life my partner's—De Bertrand's—granddaughter, d'ye understand me? because that reason was added to the others."

"No, not quite, Monsieur, not quite," Robe said, contemptuously, eying his antagonist from head to toe; "I don't consider that I understand you."

Nor did he, indeed; for this man in passion was so different from what he ordinarily was; he who was wont to be masterful now lost that self-mastery; and about them were the singing shot. But Lafitte went on:

"Of course, I had an object,—a weakness. It was that she would not approve of the position I held. It was she, Monsieur, as much as any other consideration; she, whose regard I had won in some small degree, could not think of me as the pirate Lafitte,—d'ye hear? It was she, and I do not deny it."

He paused, his passion seemingly expressed by that lurid scene.

"And yet you, a boy from Virginia, dare to come between us. I'll not have it, Monsieur; I'll not have it."

Robe said:

"It matters not to me what you will have and what not, Monsieur. The tenor of your talk is extremely distasteful, d'you understand? It is between her and me."

"If you find it distasteful, there's the alternative, Monsieur," said the other, advancing a step,—"there's the alternative."

"I know it, and shall accept it, Monsieur, when your second waits on me," said Robe, bowing. A shell rushed through the sky. He looked at the men working in the mud and dirt, and at Lafitte, their leader.

"You have heard me," he said, turning on his heel. "You have heard me."

But Lafitte did not reply. His chin rested on his hand, looking out over the scene.

Captain Robe turned and left him, feeling that he hated this man and gladly would meet him.

CHAPTER XIX

OTHER DAYS OF BATTLE

In the morning, clear, frosty, resplendent with the low southeasterly sun, we saw a great mass of scarlet-coated men approaching,—fine, with accurate step,—such an exhibition of military pomp and power as Robe never had seen. And then suddenly was a loud report, and the Chalmette houses were blown up; a shell had fallen in powder stores. And that obstruction being removed, the splendid, advancing mass saw the stern throats of the Yankee guns, which burst out in a hoarse refrain of terror and destruction. The aide, watching at this moment beside the general in the dormer window of the Macarty house, saw the scarlet coats tumbling, falling, and yet advancing; and then it all seemed to bend and fall.

"This is not the Peninsula, Robe," said

the Tennesseean, turning to the young Virginian, of whom he was fond.

Then there was the New Year's Eve, 1815, and we saw, facing us, three demilunes, equidistant from each other, and many pieces of heavy ordnance, served we knew by the best gunners, who had been trained by the greatest captains.

Then a scurrying mist hid them from view.

We were having a parade that day, our uniforms brushed, our accoutrements diligently polished, the bands playing merrily " Yankee Doodle ;" and they stood expectant behind the fog, which suddenly lifted, when a hail of shot and shells assailed and shook us.

" To your posts !" came the orders.

We slipped to our places. The general seemed everywhere, waving his cap,—now encouraging one, now the other. And our guns gave them a response.

" The cotton bales ! the cotton bales !" cried a voice. " Quick, captain !"

Those unfortunate bales had been lighted by a shot and were blazing. We tumbled them out, and Robe so burnt his right hand that he had to carry it to a surgeon. But our weakness in the burning bales was corrected.

And that tremendous cannonading kept up, but the reply was less frequent from the other side, and the smoke rising, we saw their works levelled and men retreating.

And so day after day passed; days that wore out the nerves and strength of both sides; fierce, terrible days,—leading to the great day.

On the seventh we heard, somewhat dismayed, that they had been reinforced by General Lambert with the Seventh Fusiliers and the Forty-third. But some moments after this the Kentuckians, twenty-three hundred strong, came in. After a march of fifteen hundred miles they, tattered and torn, had reached New Orleans, where the citizens clothed and fed them.

So our dismay was lessened. On the left bank of the river we had four thousand good and now tried men; on the right of the river were Generals Coffee and Ross, whose men

CHALMETTE

were knee deep in the water during the day, and at night snatched uncertain sleep at some dry point, or even on a floating log.

Back of us at intervals of two miles were reserves made up of the less able of us.

In front we had strengthened our bulwarks and looked carefully to our guns.

So came the eighth of January, 1815.

CHAPTER XX

THE EIGHTH OF JANUARY

Captain Robe, asleep in a ditch, was wakened by a rough shake. An eager face looked down at him. He raised himself, rubbing his eyes.

"La Roux!" said he, on his feet.

"Hist, captain," La Roux said; "don't call out my name that loud. I am, captain, a traitor."

"A traitor, Monsieur La Roux!" our captain cried.

"Not so loud, Monsieur Captain,—not so loud. Would you have me killed?"

"No, my good fellow,—how absurd! I never have had anything but kindness at your hands since you made us prisoners at Barataria."

"Yes, and I liked you, Monsieur,—from the first,—from the first. And she——"

He bent his head and spoke almost as if ashamed.

"I was brought up to our trade, as our great Captain de Bertrand was. I never knew aught else, Monsieur, till Monsieur Jean Lafitte persuaded me to give up the work at sea for that he had to do at Barataria. Since then I have been for the most in Louisiana. My father had naught to say to me; my mother was a Carthaginian woman, whom he discarded. Yet blood is thicker than water, Monsieur; she is of my line——"

"She?" asked Robe, almost bewildered. "You can't mean——"

"Yes, your Mademoiselle Maurice is my half-niece, Monsieur. I am Captain de Bertrand's natural son. And——"

"You are her relative," Robe said, taking the little man's thin, narrow hand.

"Yes, Monsieur,—her relative. And I have eyes. Jean Lafitte has thought too much of her, I know. And you think much of her, Monsieur. And I say,—because a hurt to you would be a hurt to her,—I say, have a care, Monsieur Captain. Jean Lafitte can strike."

For a moment he paused, and the irregular firing along the lines timed Robe's thoughts.

"Have a care, Monsieur!"

And La Roux vanished into the gloom that was lighting with the day.

He meant then that his leader would do Robe a harm. Robe laughed, and yet in some way was concerned. Yet what harm, should he wish it, could Lafitte do? He had challenged him and had received no response. In his busy days he had no chance of seeing him. But La Roux knew his master; and La Roux had warned him. He would have his eyes opened.

And the dawn was over the works, and a great scarlet line was marching on, on, a blaze of rockets before; the assault had come at last; there was Gibbs's and Keane's divisions, and Sir Edward himself close under our lines, and our guns were belching out,—belching out. And the general's voice sounded shrill and commanding:

"Stand to your guns! See that every shot tells!"

And again Robe heard him,—

"Give it to them, boys!"

What an uproar, what a furious pandemonium! the whole line seemed to be pelting fire. The Tennesseeans, keen, alert, stood on the wall, not minding their exposure,—indeed, making every shot tell.

The red, human mass shook and waved, and yet came on, till they seemed not two hundred yards away.

"Fire! Fire!" Robe heard the shout.

And with what precision of perfect discipline was that order obeyed! A line of men would fall, to be replaced by another. And we followed our general's order to the letter, not wasting a shot. Never has Robe seen a more fearful nor yet a more splendid sight. He could see no less a personage than Sir Edward himself leading a regiment of Highlanders close behind,—the Forty-fourth, as it was to prove. On they came, men dropping here and there, perhaps some rising again, but, for the most, staying there, crushed by that storm of fire and lead. For the Tennesseeans were unerring in their aim, not a shot failing. 'Twas a marksmanship that gained Napoleon's commendation. And the Baratarians and the crews of the "Carolina" and the "Louisiana" were as sure at their big guns. Robe saw the brave Sir Edward's horse's fall, and he mounted a little pony a young officer offered him. And the column kept on. But no endurance could meet that dreadful fire. The column was broken and cast down. You could almost hear in your imagination the voices of the officers. But again they rose with a stern defiance, their lips framing their Highland cries. The conquerors of many a field were not to be so beaten back by these wild, uncouth men they saw on the bulwarks. Tossing aside knapsacks and useless equipments, they advanced again. One at least had a charmed life,—brandishing his sword, a fine, smooth-faced man, proud in his strength and his determination. A sharpshooter cursed lustily; his skill seemed to fail him. That leader and a half-dozen others were to the parapet's foot; the young officer with a spring was on the top, calling back to his followers; and then with a convulsive leap he fell over into Captain Robe's arms. And Robe laid him down and felt a sob in his own heart. And he turned again to his duty. For that was the day when there could be no pause, no rest.

And still they were advancing, and still were being cut down, like a great field of poppies bending under the scythe.

"That was Pakenham," said M. St. Gême, excitedly, in Robe's ear. Yes, Pakenham had fallen, than whom no leader was ever braver. But the disorganized force again seemed to rally, again bore onward with British sullenness. Again an officer is on the parapet, and Cafferty, who is at that point, telling him he is too brave to die. "Tell my commander I fell on your parapet," Major Wilkinson, says and dies. And back there they are breaking,—the survivors, for whole regiments have been swept away. And the reserve comes up only to cover what is a sorry, despairful, angry flight from those fearful guns and rifles.

"How long d'ye think it has been?" Cafferty asks Robe.

"Two hours," said the other,—"two hours easily."

"Why, man, it's been just twenty-five minutes."

The smoke scurried about and hid the field. Our firing slackened, and you could hear in English and French, as the hot, grimy men felt their success. And the bands burst out with a great clamor of "Hail, Columbia." But as the scurrying smoke left the field, we turned from exultation almost to dismay. Such a field as that Robe never may see again,—such a crime of war! For a quarter of a mile bodies were packed together, some still, some trying to crawl away. And these were the fine, smoothly-shaven soldiers of the King of Great Britain,—our cousins in blood and tradition.

Presently a trumpeter appears, a private with a white flag, an officer beside him. Captain Robe is detailed to meet him.

"I have this letter for General Jackson," says the officer.

CHALMETTE 247

"I will deliver it, sir," and Robe pauses. "I never could have imagined greater stubbornness,—to rush on in the face of that fire."

"Sir Edward is dead; General Keane and General Gibbs badly wounded," says the officer. "My God, sir, it's terrible,—horrible! But we must have time to bury our dead. Across the river it went better with us."

Robe bows an acknowledgment to that little pardonable pride; a brave man's suffering touches even the victor; we so easily might have been the conquered.

Our general reads the letter carefully, with no exultation in his manner.

"Call the officer's attention, Captain Robe, to the fact that the sender of this note has not designated his authority."

The letter comes back shortly, duly signed:

"John Lambert, Commander-in-Chief of His Majesty's forces in Louisiana."

And we go down to help them, to assist as best we can, while the armistice lasts.

All that afternoon was taken up with those gruesome details. It was hard to think these men were dead. Our prisoners and wounded were sent to the city,—where already a young creole gentleman had ridden wildly in, shouting:

"Victory! Victory!"

And why a victory! If those fighters had known the peace had been signed before the fight began, the lives of two thousand six hundred men had been saved on the British and a score on our side. A pity, indeed, you say. Ah, yes, a pity. But, then, the prestige of our arms was established; we gave it back to them for the burning of Washington. Yet,—Robe is an old man now, his fine enthusiasms are gone, and it seems as if the price of our glory was too costly. He remembers that night when by flaring torches the dead were buried by hundreds in the garden of Villeré's.*

---

* [My dear grandfather with his usual modesty fails to relate what everybody knows, that, aide though he was, he led a most decisive little charge on one of the earlier days, which, indeed, gained him his colonelcy. His extreme reticence in speaking about his own personal achievements is provoking to his editor, who knows that even in the Battalion d'Orleans, so distinguished on the Day of Chalmette, there was no braver, more efficient officer than Christopher Robe.—C. R. F.]

CHAPTER XXI

THE QUARREL OF M. JEAN LAFITTE AND CAPTAIN ROBE

WHAT Robe has to relate now in his own story is indeed most exasperating. For to go through a great battle without a scar, and then to have a wound from another dastardly cause certainly is not distinguishing, and one may cry out on such a fate. The openly avowed antagonism of Jean Lafitte has been told of in that little less than remarkable talk our captain had with Lafitte when one day carrying an order to Captain Dominique You. The warning and extraordinary statement of La Roux had followed. But in the activity of those busy, tired days there had been little time to consider what these things meant. Would Lafitte, out of some pique and jealousy, after he had confessed that the Virginia girl had partly induced his course of action,

—would he descend to some low rascal's means of revenge? Yet the man's character was made up of so many different qualities; —those of the fine gentleman, those of the leader of buccaneers. In gaining his position he had used all the means a desperate man may. So you cannot say that what Robe here has to tell for the first time was so surprising.

'Twas the night of the eighth. General Jackson, much chagrined at a most disgraceful retreat made by ours on the right bank of the river, had sent Captain Robe with an escort of three men to investigate the causes. Now, as the captain was stepping into the boat there came a shot from somewhere; it might have been a chance shot; it might have been purposeful. For who could tell, —in that body of men we had many from conditions that are hard to imagine in these days of the United States.

Did you ever know what it is to have a wound? Robe was to have another in Mexico,—years after; that was in battle; this, too, perhaps, was in battle. The armistice was already ended. But, however it came, Robe was shot, though he knew not how. It was as if some frightful blow had been struck him: there was a faintness, and consciousness passed. Nor did he know himself until many days after; and he awoke in a still, white room, where all that was heard was a clock ticking and a voice intoning a negro melody. His strength was not even equal to raising his voice, and gradually his eyes closed again; and there were looking down on him a quadroon, red-turbaned, and a white-headed old man, who was saying,—

"He will be better now, Mademoiselle. The fever has passed."

And there answered another voice, low and musical; and the eyes he wished to see looked down into his. And he wished to speak, but she said, "Hush, dear," and she bent over and kissed him.

And then after some more hours he said, "Is it you, indeed, Sallie? I thought I was far away in a swamp, and they were fighting, —fighting. It was horrible."

"It is I, Kit, dear. But it was a glorious victory."

Then he began to understand, to remember it all, from first to last; and then he thought of Lafitte's face as he had talked with him that time by the guns. And then came all those reflections with which this chapter begins,—about Lafitte's character. Had the Baratarian leader been behind that shot out of the gloom? Had the warning of La Roux been well founded? And one day he asked her,—how many things they were to talk of as he lay there! how many confidences and confessions they were to exchange!—

"How did I get here, dear? It is Madame Demarche's, isn't it?"

"Yes, Madame Demarche's, in the city. Do you not suppose I inquired about you, Kit? Oh, how we worried when those guns sounded all day,—day after day,—till it came to the last day. That morning the Ursulines put over their chapel the image of Our Lady of Prompt Succor, and prayed to her,—and she and God heard,—even if you be a Protestant, Kit, you must allow. And, indeed, all the city prayed.

"But when the wounded were brought in we all tried what we could do to help, and no one worked better than that little Marie de Renier you made love to so furiously, Kit."

"I have confessed it," said he.

"Oh, have you? But hush, don't talk. Every house in New Orleans was turned into a hospital, and every woman into a nurse, and we have tried to take care of those poor, brave fellows whom we defeated. But among all I was expecting,—whom do you think? Can't you imagine, Kit? Then Mr. Lafitte came here very calm and serious, and he asked to have you brought here. He said you had been shot and were delirious. And he had you brought here, looking to you very carefully, Kit."

"Jean Lafitte! Jean Lafitte!" the invalid said. Had he wronged the man, then?

"No one could have been more thoughtful; no one could have done more for you."

And Robe was silent, wondering over his false suspicions.

"That was five weeks ago, Monsieur Robe," she said, smiling at him. "And you were very, very ill,—a fearful fever. And what you raved about would fill a book. And I discovered that you were jealous."

"Of Lafitte?"

"Yes, of him. You told all your secrets."

"And you still believe in me, Sallie?"

"Oh, I like you as well, though I was shocked once or twice. No matter, dear; but you must get rid of these notions about Mr. Lafitte. No one in the world could have been,—could be,—nicer to you and to me."

"Five weeks," said Robe; "I have been here all that time." He did not wish to say more that moment about the Baratarian. But Sallie continued the subject with a great show of interest.

"And all the Baratarians have been pardoned, and Captain Dominique You has been publicly thanked by General Jackson for his service at the guns. Listen, Kit, to this proclamation by the President."

She took a paper from a table and read:

"Offenders who have refused to become associates of the enemy in war upon the most seducing terms of invitation, and who have aided to repel this hostile invasion of the territory of the United States, can no longer be considered as other than objects of general forgiveness."

She threw the sheet down and looked at the invalid.

"Isn't that fine? And it puts me in not so bad a position before your uncle."

"I consult you and myself on that point," Robe said,—" no other soul in the world."

He was thinking of what Lafitte had said in that moment of self-revealing passion,— that he partly had taken his position because that would please Captain de Bertrand's granddaughter. And then she was really in a degree responsible for the pardon of Barataria, for the good service we ill could have spared on the Day of Chalmette; a woman in this case, then, and she so finely charming. Was it true that he who had given to Ronald the fair chance of the duel could have resorted to an assassin's way,—out of that same self-confessed passion? And why then had he brought his wounded enemy direct to her whom it was all about? Why had he been to such particular pains to atone for what he had done,—if he, indeed, had done it? It seemed, after all, little likely that he had. The burden of evidence was the other way.

"And if there is any question of Mr. Lafitte's full social recognition, you must know that he has been asked to serve with M. de St. Gême, whose name itself is a passport, as second in a duel. And, oh, Kit, you have missed so many balls, so many dances!"

"You are in the spirit of dancing, I notice," he said, "which you weren't some time ago."

"You have made me so," she said, "by getting better."

"And that is worth having been very ill to hear." And he said some things which need not be written here.

"Was the army well received?" he asked, at last.

"Well received; I should say so," Sallie went on. "Poor boy, I could no more enjoy it than you could. But I will tell you about it. They put up an arch in the Place d'Armes. And then they had the handsomest women in New Orleans,—you know how handsome they can be, you susceptible Kit. One was Liberty, the other Justice, standing by the pillars at each side of the arch. At their sides two children held laurel wreaths. Then from the arch to the cathedral there were two lines of your beauties, Kit, with behind each one an upright lance with the arms of a State or a Territory. Flowers and evergreens were about the arch, you know, and extended in festoons from lance point to lance point and over the street to the cathedral, where the door was finely decorated with flowers. This was January twenty-third, you know, Kit."

"And I lost myself on the eighth."

"On the great eighth, Kit, dear, which all this celebration was about."

"Well, such a crowd! Ah, if you could have seen it. Then the general, ugly and handsome all at once,—I saw him from the balcony,—came into the city by the river gate, his staff behind him,—save one import tant member, dear Kit, who was struggling with his wound and the fever. Then the guns roar; they made me shudder, thinking how many were killed by them on the eighth; and the bands are a-playing, and the people —black and white—are shouting; and the cherubs at the arch's foot are crowning him with a laurel wreath. Then he passes under the arch, and is met by Louisiana, who says something like, 'Hail, hero!' don't you know, my Christopher? It was a prettily worded speech, they say. Then when he descends, all the United States, the beauties, Kit, throw flowers for him to walk on; and at the cathedral door stands the Abbé Dubourg, with a line of priests behind; and the abbé makes a speech, and the general replies, they say, as if he had done nothing at all,—as if anybody could have saved New Orleans, which I thought very modest and proper. Then he goes into the cathedral and the Battalion d'Orleans behind him, and the 'Te Deum' rises grandly, Madame Demarche says; and after all is over there are dinners, and in the evening fireworks and balls,—

such balls! Marie de Renier says. She is very much followed up by a Lieutenant Beaumont,* one of the prisoners; you may not like to hear, Kit."

"I am terribly troubled," he said,—"terribly, dear Sallie. And you went to no balls, Sallie?"

"You were ill, Kit," she said; and there was some more said, which need not be written here.

And as the invalid grew stronger there came others with many stories,—Cafferty, Deschamps, M. de St. Gême, Captain Dominique You, even General Jackson himself, who told his aide of the victory very modestly indeed; what a shame Sir Edward Pakenham's death was! what a masterly retreat General Lambert made!

Then one day came John Robe, of Westmore, who, despite his gout, had journeyed to see his nephew, of whom he seemed quite proud. Now may Robe state that his uncle

---

* Mademoiselle de Renier married this Lieutenant—later Admiral Beaumont, and later Earl of Rutven.—C. R. F.

was not so strenuous in his opposition to his marriage when he heard that Miss Maurice had inherited a great fortune. 'Tis strange how riches will destroy a prejudice, how even very good men—of lineage to be very proud of—will swallow their prejudices when a fortune is concerned;* how Kit's uncle forgot the bad blood of Miss Maurice. And, indeed, weren't these piratical folk all pardoned?

And among others there came to see the convalescent a certain little fellow, La Roux.

"I'm sorry," said he; "I told you to be careful."

"You don't mean that it really was Jean Lafitte who shot me, or caused me to be shot?"

"I certainly do," La Roux said. "But you through her will become in some sense my kin. So I warned you, but too late, Monsieur,—too late."

"I seem to be recovering," said Robe.

---

* I may state that my grandmother's fortune was always liberally spent in charities. It was quite dissipated by my family in trying to support the cause of the Confederacy.—C. R. F.

"Oh, well-a-day, he was sorry for it,—after it was done. Yes, sorry. Good-bye, captain."

And the young man extended his hand, which Robe pressed.

"You are going away?"

"I am going again into the service of Carthagena."

"Into the Gulf trade?" Robe asked. "Why,—when you are well out of it?"

"Ask why the bird flies?" La Roux said. "My nature, captain, the nature my father gave me. And I never have betrayed my position,—never, save this once to you, and that's a question of kinship. Good-bye, Captain Robe."

And he went out, leaving Robe thoughtful. Yet scarcely had he gone before the door opened, and Madame Demarche came in, in her usual bustling way.

"He is quite able to see you, Monsieur, my dear Monsieur."

And there stood Jean Lafitte, extremely well tailored,—his face firm, strong, suave, —repeating polite commonplaces to the invalid. But when Madame had gone, he turned quickly, his eyes flashing, and he said:

"You have, Captain Robe, satisfaction to ask of me?"

Robe studied him for a moment.

"You shot me,—or had me shot, Monsieur Lafitte?"

"Yes, yes."

"Why then afterward did you try to save my life?"

"It was for her, not for you; I knew it would hurt her."

"It was true,—what you told me,—that her position led you or influenced you in refusing the British overtures?"

"Quite true, Monsieur."

"Monsieur Lafitte," said Robe then, "I have no quarrel with you. You are a strange man,—a strange combination of one given to a rascal's methods and of a gentleman. You have served her, and you have served me; and you have served the United States. You have done me one injury, 'tis true. But, as the aggrieved party,

CHALMETTE 263

'tis for me to prove the quarrel. Monsieur, I have no quarrel with you."

"I am obliged, Monsieur," Lafitte said, bowing; and he went out of the room.

A few moments after the door opened and Sallie Maurice was there.

"Mr. Lafitte bade you good-bye?" she said.

"Yes," he said. "Why?"

"He has left New Orleans, he says, forever. He goes to Galveston."

"Are you sorry, dear?" Robe asked, almost if not quite suspiciously.

"Why, Kit, I believe you are jealous now," she said, leaning towards him. And here was another episode that need not be recorded here.

But neither of those two saw Lafitte again. Both he and his brother Pierre disappeared from New Orleans in the hey-day of their reputation. Jean afterwards was engaged in privateering at Galveston and about the Gulf, where he boasted of carrying again Carthaginian letters of marque, and there's a report that he died an admiral in that service. It was asserted that in his latter years he became very boldly unscrupulous; that he did not hesitate to commit serious crimes. Robe often asked Dominique You about him. Captain You remained in New Orleans, where he died in prosperity and the enjoyment of an excellent civic reputation. But of the brothers Lafitte and of La Roux he would say nothing. And, however unscrupulous Lafitte may have been, he turned over religiously to Philip Maurice all the great De Bertrand property, consisting very largely of valuable estates in city and country.

'Tis, my children, a far cry to those times, when buccaneering so considerably influenced the history of an American Commonwealth; —when the mighty battle of Chalmette was fought and won.

THE END.

BY

ANNE HOLLINGSWORTH WHARTON.

Through Colonial Doorways.

With a number of colonial illustrations from drawings specially made for the work. 12mo. Cloth, $1.25.

"It is a pleasant retrospect of fashionable New York and Philadelphia society during and immediately following the Revolution; for there was a Four Hundred even in those days, and some of them were Whigs and some were Tories, but all enjoyed feasting and dancing, of which there seemed to be no limit. And this little book tells us about the belles of the Philadelphia meschianza, who they were, how they dressed, and how they flirted with Major André and other officers in Sir William Howe's wicked employ."—*Philadelphia Record.*

Colonial Days and Dames.

With numerous illustrations. 12mo. Cloth, $1.25.

"In less skilful hands than those of Anne Hollingsworth Wharton's, these scraps of reminiscences from diaries and letters would prove but dry bones. But she has made them so charming that it is as if she had taken dried roses from an old album and freshened them into bloom and perfume. Each slight paragraph from a letter is framed in historical sketches of local affairs or with some account of the people who knew the letter writers, or were at least of their date, and there are pretty suggestions as to how and why such letters were written, with hints of love affairs, which lend a rose-colored veil to what were probably every-day matters in colonial families."—*Pittsburg Bulletin.*

For sale by all Booksellers, or will be sent, post-paid, upon receipt of price,

J. B. LIPPINCOTT COMPANY, Publishers,
PHILADELPHIA.

Mrs. A. L. Wister's Translations.

12mo.   Cloth, $1.00 per volume.

COUNTESS ERIKA'S APPRENTICESHIP	By Ossip Schubin.
"O THOU, MY AUSTRIA!"	By Ossip Schubin.
ERLACH COURT	By Ossip Schubin.
THE ALPINE FAY	By E. Werner.
THE OWL'S NEST	By E. Marlitt.
PICKED UP IN THE STREETS	By H. Schobert.
SAINT MICHAEL	By E. Werner.
VIOLETTA	By Ursula Zoge von Manteufel.
THE LADY WITH THE RUBIES	By E. Marlitt.
VAIN FOREBODINGS	By E. Oswald.
A PENNILESS GIRL	By W. Heimburg.
QUICKSANDS	By Adolph Streckfuss.
BANNED AND BLESSED	By E. Werner.
A NOBLE NAME	By Claire von Glümer.
FROM HAND TO HAND	By Golo Raimund.
SEVERA	By E. Hartner.
A NEW RACE	By Golo Raimund.
THE EICHHOFS	By Moritz von Reichenbach.
CASTLE HOHENWALD	By Adolph Streckfuss.
MARGARETHE	By E. Juncker.
TOO RICH	By Adolph Streckfuss.
A FAMILY FEUD	By Ludwig Harder.
THE GREEN GATE	By Ernst Wichert.
ONLY A GIRL	By Wilhelmine von Hillern.
WHY DID HE NOT DIE?	By Ad. von Volckhauser.
HULDA	By Fanny Lewald.
THE BAILIFF'S MAID	By E. Marlitt.
IN THE SCHILLINGSCOURT	By E. Marlitt.
COUNTESS GISELA	By E. Marlitt.
AT THE COUNCILLOR'S	By E. Marlitt.
THE SECOND WIFE	By E. Marlitt.
THE OLD MAM'SELLE'S SECRET	By E. Marlitt.
GOLD ELSIE	By E. Marlitt.
THE LITTLE MOORLAND PRINCESS	By E. Marlitt.

"Mrs. A. L. Wister, through her many translations of novels from the German, has established a reputation of the highest order for literary judgment, and for a long time her name upon the title-page of such a translation has been a sufficient guarantee to the lovers of fiction of a pure and elevating character, that the novel would be a cherished home favorite. This faith in Mrs. Wister is fully justified by the fact that among her more than thirty translations that have been published by Lippincott's there has not been a single disappointment. And to the exquisite judgment of selection is to be added the rare excellence of her translations, which has commanded the admiration of literary and linguistic scholars."—*Boston Home Journal.*

J. B. LIPPINCOTT COMPANY, PHILADELPHIA.

By Mrs. Lindon W. Bates.

Bunch-Grass Stories.

12mo. Cloth, $1.25.

There is uncommon freshness, like a wind from the wide plains, in these tales called *Bunch-Grass Stories*. They are the work of a writer who observes and seizes the picturesque traits in every land where fortune happens to call her, and her travels have evidently been many and far away. She has, likewise, much reading, which she puts to good account in stories that impart the ring of truth to classic episodes.

A Blind Lead.

The Story of a Mine.

12mo. Cloth, $1.25.

"'A Blind Lead' is certainly a powerful book. We took it up indifferently enough, but we had read a few pages only before we found it was no ordinary work by no ordinary writer. A good deal of skill is shown in the drawing of character. There are no dull pages, and the interest is continuous from the first chapter to the last."—*Boston Advertiser.*

A Nameless Wrestler.

12mo. Paper, 50 cents; cloth, $1.00.

"Her story, 'A Blind Lead,' was very promising, and it is followed by an extremely interesting tale, 'A Nameless Wrestler.' Here is something outside the hackneyed course of fiction—fresh, strong, fascinating, dramatic, and wholesome—scenes laid in an unfamiliar country, though our own, and characters human enough to be all the more interesting because touched with strange traits by virtue of environment."—*Detroit Tribune.*

J. B. LIPPINCOTT COMPANY, PHILADELPHIA.

Fate at the Door.
A NOVEL.
By Jessie Van Zile Belden.

12mo. Paper, 50 cents; crushed buckram, ornamental, $1.00.

"The story is decidedly clever, and the semi-flirtatious relations of society men and women are admirably, wittily described."—*Boston Literary World.*

"This is a story of more than a little originality, a thoughtful and well-told story."—*Boston Courier.*

"An admirably written story, instinct with ethical suggestion."—*Philadelphia Press.*

"There is a true womanliness about this story of the social world that leaves a delightful impression upon the reader."—*Boston Herald.*

"Each page is turned with regret, since it brings one nearer to the end of the charming book."—*Amusement Gazette*, Cleveland, Ohio.

"It is one of those novels one is glad to have read, one which is remembered for a long time, and one which thoroughly awakens the emotions."—*New York World.*

"This is a strong, pathetic, eloquent little story, and one which will be remembered by its readers long after many more pretentious novels have passed to the limbo of things forgotten. 'Fate at the Door' is not a book to be allowed to go unread."—*News*, Charleston, S. C.

"To make its treatment perfectly effective, a story treating with the problem of platonic love requires high literary skill and great delicacy, and these Mrs. Belden has displayed to a remarkable height of genius. This novel alone entitles her to rank among the finest and most interesting writers of the day."—*Boston Home Journal.*

"A very interesting story, in which the movement is quick and effective and the characters are well handled. It is a story of misplaced affection which could be placed elsewhere without difficulty or risk of repulsion if it were not restrained by strong moral convictions."—*Buffalo Commercial.*

J. B. LIPPINCOTT COMPANY, PHILADELPHIA.

www.ingramcontent.com/pod-product-compliance
Lightning Source LLC
Chambersburg PA
CBHW032006230426
43672CB00010B/2272